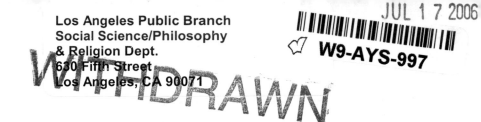

WE WON'T BACK DOWN
Severita Lara's Rise from
Student Leader to Mayor

Also by José Angel Gutiérrez

A Chicano Manual on How to Handle Gringos

A Gringo Manual on How to Handle Mexicans

*The Making of a Civil Rights Leader:
José Angel Gutiérrez*

*They Called Me "King Tiger": My Struggle for
the Land and Our Rights*

WE WON'T BACK DOWN
Severita Lara's Rise from Student Leader to Mayor

José Angel Gutiérrez

PIÑATA
BOOKS

Arte Público Press
Houston, Texas

This volume is made possible through grants from the Charles Stewart Mott Foundation, the Ewing Marion Kauffman Foundation, the Rockefeller Foundation; the Exemplar Program, a program of Americans for the Arts in Collaboration with the LarsonAllen Public Services Group, funded by the Ford Foundation, and the City of Houston through The Cultural Arts Council of Houston / Harris County.

Recovering the past, creating the future

Arte Público Press
University of Houston
452 Cullen Performance Hall
Houston, Texas 77204-2004

Cover design by James F. Brisson
Photos courtesy of José Angel Gutiérrez

Gutiérrez, José Angel.
    We Won't Back Down: Severita Lara's Rise From Student Leader to Mayor / José Angel Gutiérrez.
        p.   cm.
    ISBN-10: 1-55885-459-2 (alk. paper)
    ISBN-13: 978-1-55885-459-8
    1. Lara, Severita, 1952- 2. Mayors—Texas—Crystal City—Biography. 3. Women mayors—Texas—Crystal City—Biography. 4. Mexican American women—Texas—Crystal City—Biography. 5. Mexican Americans—Civil rights—Texas—Crystal City—History—20th century. 6. Civil rights movements—Texas—Crystal City—History—20th century. 7. Student movements—Texas—Crystal City—History—20th century. 8. Crystal City (Tex.)—Ethnic relations. 9. Crystal City (Tex.)—Politics and government. 10. Crystal City (Tex.)—Biography. I. Title.
F394.C83G895   2005
976.4′437′0092—dc22   2005046245
[B]   CIP

⊛ The paper used in this publication meets the requirements of the American National Standard for Information Sciences—Permanence of Paper for Printed Library Materials, ANSI Z39.48-1984.

5 6 7 8 9 0 1 2 3 4   10 9 8 7 6 5 4 3 2 1

Table of Contents

To Severita Lara, thank you for all you did, have done, and continue to do for La Raza.

To my daughters, Andrea and Clavel, that you both rise to leadership roles and learn to stand up, taste victory, negotiate, find yourself, and serve generations yet to come.

And, thank you, Chicanas everywhere for your strength.

Foreword

The 1960s and 1970s spawned some of the most significant Hispanic civil rights and social justice activities in U.S. history. During these years, Americans gained unprecedented exposure to the plight of Spanish-speaking people in the United States, through the organizing activities of Hispanic workers, students, artists, and community activists.

Perhaps the most intellectually driven figure of the leading Mexican American—or Chicano[1]—activist of these years was José Angel Gutiérrez. Gutiérrez, a community and political organizer from South Texas who went on to become an attorney and a prolific writer, spearheaded a new vehicle to radically alter Mexican-American political participation. It was called the Raza Unida ("United People's") Party. During the early 1970s, the Raza Unida Party succeeded against overwhelming odds to win key elected offices in and around Crystal City, Texas, which helped to change the face of U.S. Hispanic politics in important ways.

Gutiérrez's political activities produced a new generation of Latino and Latina political leadership, not all of which remained active in the Raza Unida Party. Some principals in this leadership went on to become active in the nation's major political parties, and many went on to play important roles in the U.S. Latino community's mainstream political evolution.

Among the untold stories of this epoch in U.S. history is that of Severita Lara, a Gutiérrez protégée who became an unlikely student leader during the informing years of the Chicano

---

[1] 'Chicano' is the term that politicized Mexican Americans (especially youth) gave themselves during the late 1960s and early 1970s.

Movement. With increasingly hard work and commitment, over a period of three decades, Lara evolved from student activist to elected politician in her home town of Crystal City, one of south Texas's most important centers of gravity relative to Latino political empowerment.

An early and close, but finally unsuccessful run for county judge against a powerful Anglo incumbent suggested seemingly insurmountable barriers to Lara's political career, which took her out of public life for nearly a decade. But then—and despite large doses of lingering institutional racism and sexism directed to her candidacy—Lara resumed her political activities and gained a successful two-term run on the Crystal City governing council. In 1995 she became mayor of Crystal City.

This recount of Lara's story by José Angel Gutiérrez underscores the important role that women played in the political development of Hispanic peoples in the decades that defined the Latino civil rights struggle in America. Too rarely told, stories like Lara's reveal an order of strength, wisdom, and engagement among Latinas that has not been sufficiently covered in historical treatments of the Hispanic civil rights experience.

We are pleased to present this key aspect of the Chicano Movement years as an important entry in Arte Público Press's Hispanic Civil Rights Book Series. The series seeks to increase public knowledge and appreciation about Hispanic contributions to U.S. civil rights advancement in the post World War II era. With generous support from funders, including the Charles Stewart Mott Foundation, the Rockefeller Foundation, the Ewing Marion Kauffman Foundation, and the James Irvine Foundation, the series has supported the public dissemination and discussion of approximately twenty new and revised works covering the key organizations and leaders that have shaped contemporary Hispanic social justice gains. By pointing out the many public achievements of these groups and individuals, even in the face of substantial mainstream resistance, the series aims to expand national comprehension of the strength and vitality of U.S. democratic institutions and of the promise of our nation's dramatically increasing cultural diversity.

José Angel Gutiérrez's *We Won't Back Down: Severita Lara's Rise from Student Leader to Mayor* presents important and insightful lessons about the many injustices Mexican Americans and other Latino people have encountered and yet largely overcome in places like Crystal City, Texas—a microcosm of the sort of town where many Hispanic Americans live and work still today across much of our nation. Based on Gutiérrez's own personal experiences and insights as an early mentor of Severita Lara, his book provides first-voice testimony to the continuing legacy of political exclusion in America. The book underscores the conditions, assumptions, and biases that produced militancy in so many, especially younger Spanish-speaking activists of the civil rights era, but which ultimately resulted in the broader mainstreaming of Latino and Latina political leaders, like Lara.

As Hispanic Americans emerge to become the nation's most populous minority group at the outset of the 21st century, many of the injustices against Hispanic people—and especially recent immigrants—sadly are on the rise. Hispanic Americans suffer continuing indignities at the hands of politicians, law enforcement officials, employers, universities, the media, philanthropic grantmaking organizations, and other leading institutions. Hispanics and especially newer immigrants are also increasingly subject to the nation's growing incidence of racially motivated hate crime.

Quite importantly, however, Gutiérrez's recount of the life of Severita Lara highlights the continuing possibilities for redemption and justice in America, even if the path to success is riddled with costs and sacrifices. In effect, what Gutiérrez is reminding us of here in the telling of Lara's story is that the continuing persistence of Latino community exclusion from the American political process is neither pre-ordained nor immune from the powerful influences of reason and social evolution. Americans of all backgrounds have the power and the opportunity to overcome our nation's sad legacy of political and civil rights injustice. We have the intellectual capacities to place our common humanity before our worst instincts and our darkest historical biases. The remaining unanswered question, however, is whether we finally have the vision and the will to do so.

José Angel Gutiérrez's book on Severita Lara—the inspiring Latina who overcame all odds to become a political force in south Texas—challenges us to address these fundamental issues. A leading protagonist of the Chicano Movement's heyday, Gutiérrez remains today a fiercely committed, although perhaps less visible and galvanizing, community advocate. His large contributions to the political and intellectual struggle for Hispanic equality in America, however, will have long-enduring impact. The work that follows reflects the reasons for this. Arte Público Press is privileged indeed to extend this important leader's contributions to the public record.

Henry A. J. Ramos
Executive Editor
Arte Público Press
Hispanic Civil Rights Book Series

WE WON'T BACK DOWN
Severita Lara's Rise from Student Leader to Mayor

Severita Lara has recalled the feelings that provoked her and her student companions to walk out of Crystal City High School:

"Eighty-five percent of the [student] population was Mexican American, yet in all of our activities, like for example, cheerleaders . . . there's always three Anglos and one mexicana. . . . We started questioning. Why should it be like that?

But the discontent went beyond extracurricular activities:

"[We] started looking at other things . . . what we're called in class . . . that mexicanos are just bandidos. . . . Whenever there were fights, it was always the mexicano that got spanked and the Anglos never did. . . . We looked at our books. There's not a nice thing about mexicanos. In class, a lot of our teachers, not all of them, would tell us we would never amount to anything. . . . And we didn't have any mexicano teachers."

Chapter 1
Cabezuda

Severita's grandparents, Modesto and Severita Lara, were political refugees from the Mexican Revolution of 1910. The Laras had come from Monclova, Nuevo León. Her grandfather Modesto was of Zapotec Indian ancestry. He was tall, dark-skinned, had black hair and eyes, and was very strong. The community saw him as a very good businessman, and very, very independent. Grandmother Severita had more Spanish than Indian blood. She was taller than Modesto with light skin and green eyes. Her grandparents met at the marketplace after Don Modesto had arrived in Monclova from Oaxaca, a southern state deeper in Mexico. After the Mexican Revolution broke out and began to reach Monclova, their respective families urged a rapid courtship and even faster marriage so the young couple could migrate to San Antonio, Texas, and be out of harm's way. It was good advice because, during the revolution, which lasted from 1910 to1930, nearly two million people died. The couple had to wait because Severita was expecting a child, Bruno, to be born in Mexico. As soon as they could travel with their new baby, they moved to Texas.

Severita and Modesto had nine children. The Lara family wanted to be closer to the border than San Antonio, so they ended up residing in Crystal City, about 45 miles from Eagle Pass, which is on the border with Piedras Negras, Coahuila. Don Modesto bought property in Crystal City in 1924. Brothers and sisters who joined him in exile also remained in Crystal City for the rest of their lives. Some of these brothers and sisters died an early death due to tuberculosis, which hit Mexican people really hard. The Lara family lost Jesusita and Modesto Jr. to the disease. At that time, there were very

1

few doctors or hospitals that cared if Mexicans were healthy or sick, lived or died. And in Crystal City there was only one Mexican doctor to care for them all. The Anglo doctors refused to treat Mexican patients.

Severita's maternal grandparents, the Cepedas, had always lived in Texas, even before the Anglos had come and taken over the Texas Republic. The Cepedas lost their lands to Anglos, but refused to move from their homeland to Mexico; instead Don Margarito, Severita's grandfather, eked out a living as a sharecropper, working someone else's land, and as a *vaquero*, or cowboy. He had a reputation in the Dilley-Millet area, south of San Antonio, Texas, for being a great farmer. He tilled the land with mules from sunup to sundown. Everything he planted came out bigger and better than his neighbors's crops, so he seldom had a problem in finding land to till, plant, and harvest.

Because the Cepedas were sharecropping farmers, they seldom stayed in one house for years at a time. They moved around the area and lived in several houses. The Cepeda boys and girls would help their dad work the land. Grandma Aurora never worked in the fields; she always stayed home to tend the farm animals they owned and do the housework. Severita's mother, Irene, went to school only to the fourth grade. She was kept at home to help care for the chickens, pigs, goats, cows, and lambs. She would also tend to the family garden plot with *chiles, cilantro, calabazita, tomates, yerba buena, cacahuates, romero, laurel, rábanos, camote, papas, maíz, zanahoria, cebolla, ajo, sandías, melones,* and fruit trees. Irene started school in Woodbury when she was eleven years old, much older than the other children in the first grade. All the children from every grade were taught together in a large one-room building at the school for Mexicans. At that time, Mexican children attended one school and Anglo children attended another. Irene felt embarrassed at being the oldest student in the first grade and, as a result, never enjoyed school.

The Mexican Revolution did not affect the Cepedas directly, as it did the Laras, but the Depression of the 1930s in the United

States did. Agricultural prices dropped, people had no money or jobs, and sharecroppers had to move off the land. Many farmers lost their land, others sold it, but most just quit farming and their field hands had to move to the cities in search of work. The Depression brought the Cepedas to Crystal City. Irene did not enroll in school in Crystal City because she was already fifteen. For all practical purposes, she was a woman at her age and did not see herself in a classroom with ten- and twelve-year-olds and teachers speaking only English to her. She quit without much schooling and little English, and never went back to school. She also did not learn city ways but remained a true farm girl, shy and ignorant of many things, though she was also a stern and austere disciplinarian. She was a hard worker and great homemaker. Fortunately, her teacher in Woodbury, Mrs. Sally Schultz, and her mother had taught her how to read in Spanish and English. Later, Irene learned English better by completing a correspondence course on the subject. She would also look up words she did not know in the dictionary while reading the newspaper.

Chemita, Don Modesto's son, married a sweetheart who had recently arrived from Mexico. The couple had promised each other to have several children. But after a few years of marriage, they remained childless. Their dreams and hopes began to turn into resentment and frustration. One day, she left the house and returned only to sign the divorce papers. Chemita threw himself into his father's businesses.

Don Modesto had bought land by the railroad tracks between North Zavala Street and North First Avenue, fronting Holland Street. He opened a bar and a fresh meat market. Later, when the demand for fresh meat made it necessary for the family to raise their own livestock, Don Modesto looked for other opportunities. On the outskirts of Crystal City toward the Nueces River, the Laras bought a small ranch on which to raise animals for the meat market. Chemita's life was divided into duties: going to and coming from the ranch to feed the animals, milk the cows, butcher the animals; tending to customers in the market during the day and the bar in the evenings; and cleaning up both market and bar late at night or very early in the morning. During the Depression, Don Modesto even began a used clothing and equipment store and rented space with tents on his land to families who had nowhere to sleep. Don Modesto had developed contacts with area farmers and was frequently asked to supply laborers, so he also became a farm labor contractor. Later, he and sons bought a gas station on the corner of Holland and North First Avenue and obtained a licensing agreement with Humble Oil and Refinery, now called Exxon. Fortunately, his sons Chemita, Bruno, and Nicolás helped with all the business endeavors and responsibilities. Don Modesto built homes for each of his sons and daughters right next to his. Each son and daughter received a forty-by-sixty-foot lot on which to build a home when he or she married.

The bar and meat market were side-by-side facing Holland Street. Chemita's lot and home were next to the businesses. Don Modesto lived in the center of the extensive property. Next to him lived Nicolás, and next to him was his sister Julia's lot. Nicolás opted for the migrant life and ended up relocating to Gilroy, California, but his home still stands on the family land in Crystal City.

Like the other brothers, Nicolás liked to drink beer and liquor, sometimes a bit too much. When any of them, sons or grandsons, came home rowdy—talking loud, making demands, and waking people up—Don Modesto would wake everybody up to witness his son's punishment. Don Modesto would make his sons and grandsons kneel in the front yard while he scolded them, humiliated them, and even hit them. To all he would announce, "If a man is going to drink, he must control his liquor, not let the liquor control him. A man who demands respect by yelling at his children or his wife is a drunk and not a real man." Severita, the granddaughter, witnessed these incidents, but she never recalled her father, Chemita, being disciplined in that way.

One day when Chemita was serving customers at the meat market, a young woman, Irene Cepeda, walked in and ordered some fresh cut. Chemita gave her an extra piece "for being so pretty," he told her. Irene was too much a country girl to even look at him; besides, he embarrassed her with such talk. She already had a boyfriend. What would he think if he heard Chemita talking this way, as did the other customers? She refused to take the coins from his hand when he handed her the change. "Put it down,"she pointed to the counter.

Chemita felt this was love at first sight, but he was troubled that she was so young. He was fifteen years older than Irene. He didn't even know her name but kept a look out for her daily. Chemita asked his brothers to help him find out who she was and where she was from. They all knew her family was not local. Chemita managed to spot her from time to time walking in the street as he drove past. He would try to make eye contact, but she either refused to return his gaze or just looked past him. At other times, he would try to engage her in conversation after greeting her at the meat market. That did not work either. She would state her business, tell him to put the change on the counter, and leave. Finally, as luck would have it, Chemita spotted Irene at the drugstore. She was with her sister Francisca. He introduced himself to her and asked if he could call on her at home.

Without hesitation, Irene looked him straight in the eye and said in Spanish, "You have no manners. Who do you think you are? Always pestering me and trying to talk to me. I have a boyfriend. What would he think? You talk to me in front of all those people at your store like you're showing off. You give me extra meat as if you are trying to bribe me. What do you think I am? You embarrass me. You want to touch my hand like a little boy."

Chemita's ears were ringing and getting really hot, as if he had a fever. Now *he* was embarrassed, because she had a loud voice and it carried. Other customers were turning and looking in their direction. As best he could, he profusely apologized to her and told her repeatedly that those were not his intentions at all. He liked her very much, he said to her, and really wanted to visit her at her home.

As quickly as she had blurted her opinion to him just seconds earlier, she responded to his forward approach, "I am not interested in you." Then she added, "But I will think about it."

Chemita started to offer his hand to shake hers but realize he was trembling and quickly put it in his pocket. He just nodded in her direction and took off without buying what he had come to get. He was so ecstatic that she had said, "But I will think about it."

Irene did think about it, very seriously. Later in life she told her daughters, Severita, Linda, Irma, and Yolanda, that she decided to marry their dad because he was a hard worker, and mature. The age difference did not bother her; in fact, she liked that because he could probably settle down. He would be a good family man to the children they would have.

Irene let Chemita know she accepted his offer of courtship. Because Chemita was divorced and the Catholic Church does not permit divorced persons to re-marry in a formal ceremony, they married in a civil ceremony at home on April 18, 1951. The lack of a church wedding did not bother the Cepeda family. Having grown up on various farms, the Cepedas did not see going to church as a regular exercise. The home wedding was not lacking in splendor and fun. They had lots of food for everyone, music played until nearly dawn, and the bridesmaids and groomsmen all wore fancy clothes.

Severita was born to the couple on February 6, 1952. Chemita wanted her named after his mother. She was a beautiful baby and a happy child. Several years in a row, the couple had another child, six in all. They had four girls and two boys: Severita, Elsa Linda, Irma Irene, José María, Yolanda, and Rolando. Rolando, the baby boy, was the only exception in the yearly births. He was born twelve years after Yolanda.

From day one, Chemita spoiled Severita. Anything Severita wanted, she got, even at times when the other children did not. Chemita would take Severita everywhere with him: to the gas station, the post office, the grocery store, the ranch, and even to the bar. Mother Irene would get livid that her child was at the bar but was helpless to do anything about it. Severita developed a love for mariachi music, dancing, and cursing in Spanish. Her mother resented the special treatment Severita received from her father and would punish her more severely and more often than the other children. When angry, Irene would grab anything—stick, hairbrush, belt, whip, board, shoe, cooking utensil, or handbag—and hit her children hard. Severita would not cry. She learned to take the punishment with the pain and not show hurt by crying. This infuriated Irene even more, and she would continue to hit Severita until she got tired. Still, Severita would not cry.

Because money was either plentiful or scarce on the sharecropper trail, she learned to make her dresses and blouses from flour sacks. She made her children all their clothes as they got older, but the girls and boys ran around the house and yard only in their underpants until they were almost six years of age. On special occasions, the family would dress up and attend an event. Irene would make Severita and Linda identical dresses. Severita hated being dressed like a twin and hated being made to dress in what her mother chose. Even at age four, she could make up her own mind and had her own tastes. Once, when her mother tried to put one of the identical dresses on her, she refused, demanding to wear another one instead. Her mother gave her no such choice and violently forced her into the dress. While her mother dressed Linda, always the compliant one, Severita marched out the door and straight into the mud puddle and rolled around. She came back into the house, got the dress she wanted and announced to her mom that she was dirty and now had to wear the other dress. Her mother was furious and gave her a beating, but Severita refused to cry. From that day on, her mother's nickname for Severita was *cabezuda*, or stubborn.

On another occasion, when photographs of students were to be taken, Severita wanted to show off her long bangs that she loved. Her mother wanted to trim them. Severita refused to let her mother cut any of her adorable bangs and started running away. Her mother was agile and quick, so she caught Severita. As punishment for running away and disobeying, her mother cut her bangs down to the scalp. Severita looked horrible. Instead of bangs flowing down, she now had hair sticking up like a boy.

When Severita reached five years of age and Linda four, Chemita placed them in the private school for Mexican children, just behind the Canela Bakery in the Mexico Grande barrio. The school was in a grocery store owned and operated by Suse Salazar, a competent teacher in both English and Spanish, whom the local public schools would not hire. Mexican parents knew the Anglo teachers would keep the Mexican children in the first grade for years until they learned English. The Anglos did not want Mexican children in the public schools, certainly not with their children. Segregated schools existed in Crystal City until the late 1950s. When integration became state and federal law, segregation was continued within the buildings by grade level. Mexican children would attend school with Anglos but be placed in all-Mexican classrooms. Just a few were placed with Anglos.

In the public schools, a child could be ten to eleven years old and only in the first grade. A few Spanish-speaking children who already knew English were still retained in the first grade to help the teacher with those who needed help with the language. The most common occurrence was for Mexican children to leave school and go to work to help their families. Compulsory attendance was not enforced. The few Mexican parents who knew both about segregation and of Suse Salazar, the alternative pre-kindergarten, paid $1.25 a week per child to learn English—its vowels, consonants, grammar, diction, vocabulary, enunciation, spelling, and writing—and basic math. Ms. Salazar, eager to make an extra dollar or two, offered Kool-Aid, ice-cube Popsicles, and other treats for a penny. For five cents the children would look into the View Master. The latter activity helped students learn geography, history, ancient folklore, mythology, and children's stories, such as "Red Riding Hood," "Mary and Her Little Lamb," "Snow White," and "Three Little Pigs." Students who attended Suse Salazar's school for at least a year learned English, perfected Spanish, could read a bit and write, and were more advanced than the Anglo children. Severita and Linda excelled; they loved to read and learn. The Anglo system had made English proficiency the locked gate to learning and knowledge. Suse Salazar's school, with a strong Spanish maintenance and bilingual education, offered the key to open that gate. Because of Suse Salazar's school, Chicano kids had a real chance at a future.

Linda and Severita often played tricks on their teacher. She had a fan that faced her and not the students, but at times Suse would doze off and Severita would turn the fan toward the students.

Each day, Chemita would drive his girls to Suse's school and pick them up in the afternoon. Severita and Linda were not much for taking naps. They were hyperactive. After school, they usually stripped down to panties and ran out the back door to the railroad tracks and to their pets. Each child had a dog. Severita at that time had a spotted pug. Linda and her bother José loved to dress their pet dogs and goats in underwear and shirts. They had a mare named Nellie that Severita would climb on, using stacked metal cans or a chair to reach up, and ride bareback.

Another favorite game was Kick the Can, or *Patada al bote*, usually played at dusk or early evening near an especially scary house. A very strange man, a hermit, lived there, just down the tracks from the Laras across Holland Street. Everyone called him *el árabe*, the Arab. His beard hung down over his chest, and his matted hair stuck out from under a greasy hat he wore pulled down to his eyes with a U.S. flag in the band. He gathered things from the streets, alleys, and garbage cans into a burlap sack he carried over his shoulder. He walked with a stick to fend off the dogs that attacked him. His house was very strange and mysterious, with a fence made out of tall sticks tied together. The corner poles of the fence and the entry gate were taller and had large bones and animal skulls tied on them. El árabe was always talking to himself and mumbling in what sounded like a foreign language. At times he would drop to the ground with face down and seemed to pray. He looked scary and was very, very dirty, and smelled really bad. Parents always told their kids to stay away from him because he ate little children. They said that the bones on the tall sticks were from children and wild animals he had eaten alive.

A dangerous game was to walk on the railroad tracks while keeping one's balance. Not easy. Other times they would place old spoons, nails, coins—any metal object—on the track for the weight of the train to flatten smooth. Another game was to see who could walk the furthest distance barefooted. Once, when they were a bit older and their mother had insisted on clothes and shoes, the girls and their cousin Viola were playing on the railroad tracks. While balancing on the track, Viola's foot got stuck. Severita could not dislodge her foot, and they could hear a train coming! In a near panic, Linda had no choice but to run home and tell her Aunt Herminia of the impending danger. But her aunt was not there. Severita stayed with Viola, tugging at the foot, shoe, and leg as the train neared. She tried and tried but could not dislodge Viola's foot. The train grew even closer, with its whistle blaring for all to get out of the way. Quickly, Irene ran back from the house, grabbed cooking oil and drenched Viola's foot and shoe. Squirt, squirt, squirt until the container was empty. Severita tugged at the leg and suddenly fell backwards when Viola's foot came out. The sock and shoe remained stuck between the two switching rails. The big, heavy train rolled by. The girls were safe.

Since nobody but the three girls knew of this near-death experience and they kept it a secret, there was no beating from Severita's mother. The beatings from their mother were no less harsh and severe as the girls got older, but they were less frequent because their mother could not catch them. Usually, Severita and Linda would hide in the outdoor toilet. It had two cut holes on a wide board and the place smelled really bad inside. Old magazine pages, brown paper, grocery bags, and newspaper were used as toilet paper. As children, Severita and her friends would see how far their butts could drop into the holes. Linda would scream with horror, begging Severita not to fall in. Severita had told Linda there were snakes and alligators down there. When they were older, they hid inside while playing games or to avoid their mother.

Later, as teenagers, when they could walk downtown and attend movies, they met boyfriends. By then, the sisters and brothers had deciphered the code words that were a prelude to a beating. When their mother said, "You've got me boiling like water for chocolate," they knew to run for cover. When she called Severita *cabezuda,* Severita knew she was targeted for a beating. The others would relax.

Every afternoon once they started regular school, their father had three family rituals with his children: he would take them for a ride in the back of his pickup every afternoon just after school and before homework and supper time; he would pray at dinner time and bedtime for his little ones; and he would tell the family a historical fact or story about Mexico. Often, the story would involve a *dicho,* or proverb, as part of the lesson. And every Christmas, Chemita had another ritual. A large box would appear underneath the Christmas tree. Only one big gift was under the tree. Chemita would sit everyone down, open the box, and read out the names of his children and pass out gifts. The gifts were all inside one box. In later years, Severita found out that her dad had made an arrangement with Oscar Rice, owner of a five-and-dime store. Chemita would take him money regularly and Mr. Rice would set aside the newest toy, doll, book, or game that came into the store and would wrap them for the Lara children. At Christmas Eve, Mr. Lara would go get the box and hide it in his truck until the early morning hours.

Christmas and birthdays were always special days at the Lara home. For birthdays there was a cake, maybe ice cream, some friends over, but not gifts. Neither her dad nor mom believed that gift giving was necessary. It was a day to be celebrated in the company of family.

As Irene had more children, she became sickly. She would not even leave the house. In fact, when the new school year rolled around, she would make every child stand on a grocery paper bag and she would outline their feet. She gave those pencil outlines to Chemita to take to the J.C. Penney store and buy each child two pairs of shoes, one for school and one for dressing up on Sundays. Irene did not even go to the grocery store; Dad and girls did. Chemita would hire household help for Irene because a family of eight was a lot to keep up with. Washing clothes for eight people was a full-day affair. Ironing was two or three days of work, plus the three meals every day, including Sundays, also meant unending work. The sweeping, dusting, washing dishes, cleaning rooms, and making beds was very taxing on Irene. The maids did not last long, because either Irene got jealous of them or Irma, the middle child, did. Only the maternal grandmother, Aurora, could say nice things about their dad.

Irene also believed in home remedies and *curanderos*, or folk healers. She made teas from herbs, usually from *ruda* or *romero*. She brushed the evil eye, with a broom for a *limpia* or cleansing. She stroked them with an egg to remove the evil eye, illnesses, and spells. When it was a serious problem that required a powerful *curandera*, Irene would take the girls to Doña Bernardita, who cured people by making them jump over a lighted candle.

Irene was often sick as the girls were growing up, and they had to begin doing more and more of the housework. Severita hated those chores and the thought of it being only for girls. She felt that was unfair. Often Severita would coax Linda into doing her chores with bribes or threats.

Because Severita and Linda had picked up the colorful speech from the bar behind their house, confessions with the local priest about their cussing always got them several Our Fathers and Hail Marys. Linda figured out the priest's punishment scheme: regardless of the number of cusswords uttered up to about thirty, the punishment was the same. Linda always confessed to the maximum. When Severita wanted Linda to do something, she either threatened Linda with exposing her cussing to Mamá Irene, which meant a sure beating, or traded Linda spare cusswords, because Severita had not used up her quota at confession.

At regular school Severita was not only the able negotiator and figured the system out quickly, but she was also the spark plug for any team. When her male cousins or little brothers lost games at marbles or spinning tops or just got into fights and lost, it was Severita, all fifty pounds of her, who launched into a furious attack. Many a time she made larger boys quit a fight or run, and she made many others return marbles taken from her relatives. Severita would regularly beat up on her brother José Maria, or Chemita Jr., in order to get him to take out the trash. That is until he reached twelve years of age, and outweighed her by eighty pounds, and was taller by a foot.

La cabezuda was developing into a real leader: smart and feisty, not a quitter, not afraid. She was a risk taker and defiant, even to her mom. She learned to hide pain and suffer the consequences of her actions and behavior. Little did she know she would need all those skills and character traits in the years to come.

Chapter 2
The Illness

The 1963 school year began with some of the Chicano students back from their annual trek to the northern states in search of seasonal work harvesting crops. The Anglo kids went on real vacations; they were not migrant workers. Severita wondered where they went. She never saw them when school was out, sometimes only at the Guild Theatre that showed English-language movies downtown. Because Severita and Linda had attended Suse Salazar's special private school, they were allowed to be in the same class as the Anglo students.

After school began, almost every week new Chicano students would enroll. By early November all the Chicano students would finally be back in school after the harvests; they would begin leaving school as early as March every year. Severita and Linda loved to talk to them about their summer adventures up north. The migrant children would talk about the long drive north, big shopping malls, playing in snow sometimes, and making money to buy clothes, music records, and gifts for others. Severita and Linda had asked their parents to let them go with a relative to work up north, but were denied permission time and time again.

One day the fifth-grade students had just settled into their chairs behind their desks for the first period when Ms. Lanning, their teacher, proudly announced the arrival of the president of the United States, John Fitzgerald Kennedy, in Houston, Texas. Severita was ecstatic. She loved John F. Kennedy and his wife, Jacqueline. Severita knew from her father that Mrs. Kennedy could speak Spanish. Ms. Lanning told the class that she was going to try to get a television set into the classroom the next day in order to view the presidential visit to Dallas.

As it turned out, she could not get good reception for the television in the classroom. The class was disappointed. By late afternoon, the class was sleepy and tired, ready to go home, when the principal's secretary came rushing into the classroom and whispered in Ms. Lanning's ear something terrible. Ms. Lanning began to sob and weep uncontrollably as the secretary rushed out as fast as she had come into the room. Ms. Lanning composed herself enough to announce to the class that the president had been shot and killed in Dallas during lunchtime. The entire class went into shock and also began to cry. Ms. Lanning tried to calm and assure the children that everyone was safe and nothing bad was going to happen. She promised to get the class all the information by the next day. Meanwhile she instructed them to gather their things and go home. "Be sure you tell your parents that everything is going to be all right. Nothing bad will happen to our country," she urged the children.

Severita, tears streaming down her face, kept asking her classmates for details: "Who killed him? Why?" But no one knew the answers and neither did her father or mother when she got home to press them for answers. Instead, they turned on the television and saw with their own eyes the terrible assassination of the president. The same film clip was repeated and repeated. Severita had nightmares about the scenes she saw on television. She did not want to see or hear about that anymore but could not help it. Everyone was always talking about the terrible times the country was going through.

In the days that followed, Severita could not focus on schoolwork; neither could any other student. The teachers had no answers. No one knew what to make of the developing events as the whole world saw them on television. First, the president was shot. The suspected assassin, Lee Harvey Oswald, was in turn shot by Jack Ruby while in police custody. Then Ruby was arrested and sent to prison. The vice president, Lyndon Baines Johnson, from

Texas, became president and announced an immediate investigation into the assassination of President Kennedy.

Severita remembered all these events particularly clearly because she came down with a severe strep throat infection. The doctor prescribed huge pills, antibiotics, that she had difficulty swallowing—so she didn't. She would try, but ultimately she would spit them out. Her mother fussed and scolded her for not taking them.

Severita did not get better; in fact, she got worse because she did not take her antibiotics to combat the infection. The strep throat descended into her lungs and heart and stomach with every breath and swallow. She soon developed rheumatic fever, which is very serious, especially among children. Severita was only twelve years old. Her hands began to cramp and the strength in her arms and legs slowly disappeared. In fact, the muscles in her arms and legs began to shrink. She had difficulty walking and holding on to her books, pencils, and drinking from cups or glasses. She dropped everything. Her mother thought she was faking because she still would run and play and dance to music in the living room. But that was when she felt better. At school she had trouble doing schoolwork.

Just before Christmas the family took her to Piedras Negras, Mexico, to see the doctors there. Her parents felt better talking to Mexican doctors because they spoke Spanish and could be understood; besides, the medicines were cheaper in Mexico. The doctors there, Dr. González-Ríos and Dr. Lorenzo Rivera, did not have good news. Severita was diagnosed with dermatomyositis. Dr. González-Ríos wanted to be sure of their diagnosis and asked to see Severita again as soon as possible for a biopsy of muscle tissue from her leg. This turned out to be the most painful experience Severita had in her lifetime. Because the muscle tissue had to be free of any contaminants, the doctors could not give her any anesthetic. Severita had to endure the operation without painkillers. Her leg was cut open and muscle cut out. As Severita screamed out in pain, she could hear her mother beating on the operating room door trying to get in, and yelling for the doctors to stop hurting her child. Her mother fainted in the hallway from Severita's screams of pain. Several nurses and attendants had to hold Severita down during the first moments of the operation until she herself fainted from the excruciating pain.

A few days after the biopsy operation Severita's parents learned from the doctors that this disease was going to cripple Severita for life and that she probably would die at an early age. Chemita and Irene Lara could not believe their ears. How could their first born be taken from them? They insisted on a second medical opinion. Dr. Lorenzo Rivera recommended they travel with Severita to Galveston, Texas, where there was a ward of similarly afflicted children, and consult the doctors there. Dr. Lorenzo Rivera gave the Laras the muscle tissue in a jar and some medicine for Severita to begin taking immediately. The doctor said, "Make sure she takes this medicine every day. Make sure. This may be the only thing that can save her." The doctor also told them that the medicine was not sold in the United States, only in Mexico.

The Lara family quickly made arrangements for the trip to Galveston. Severita could no longer walk or hold anything in her hands. The lower halves of her legs had become very thin from atrophied muscles. Her calves had shrunk. Her arms had withered. The fingers of her hands and the toes of her feet had turned inward. She looked deformed. She had to be carried everywhere and spent her days and nights mostly in bed. Severita no longer went to school.

In Galveston after examining Severita and the biopsy, the doctors there confirmed the diagnosis of the Mexican doctors. They had been correct. The Galveston doctors also confirmed that Severita would be crippled soon. They also told the parents that she would die at an early age. Severita did not know that this was her fate. She had not been told any of this. The doctors spoke only to her parents, and her parents only told her she was going to get better. Fortunately, one doctor at the Galveston hospital took

Severita in a wheelchair to see the children in the ward with the same disease. These children were all crippled and bed-ridden. They could not walk or move their arms. They had lumps and knots on their legs and arms and bodies. Some of them had legs and arms amputated. She was horrified and scared. With tears in her eyes, Severita looked at her parents and at the doctor and said, "I am going to walk. I'm never going to be in here."

The doctor was surprised by her attitude. Calmly but firmly, he told Severita and her parents that she might have to be placed in this ward if the medicine from Mexico did not work. He also said that she had to begin an exercise program immediately, regardless if it hurt her arms and legs, otherwise she would be crippled for sure. The doctor recommended that Severita be made to exercise daily and be massaged on her legs and arms several times a day. The doctor showed both her father and mother how to do the leg and arm massage. He also recommended massage therapy from a chiropractor.

As soon as they returned to Crystal City, her father took her bicycle to a welder friend, who made it into a stationary bicycle by putting it on a metal stand and putting straps on the pedals to hold her feet in place. Severita was going to exercise on that bicycle. Her father also inquired about the best chiropractor in the area and found one in Cotulla, Texas, some forty miles in the opposite direction from Piedras Negras. They would see Dr. John Lavasick in Cotulla twice a week. Chemita would have to find a way to leave someone in charge at the gas station on Tuesdays and Thursdays. Money was going to be a problem, but somehow they would manage. Severita's mom, Irene, began trying to get Severita on the stationary bicycle. She had so much trouble with Severita. Twice daily she had to lift and carry her to the bicycle. Severita did not want to grab the handle bars or put her feet into the straps. She would cry and scream out in pain. Her mother would cry with her, but sternly made her do it every day. Mid-morning and afternoon when exercise time was due, was torture for both mother and daughter. Her mother would also massage her legs and arms every day. Severita would try to convince her mother that the massage was just as good as the exercise, so she could skip exercising, but her mother wisely refused. The easiest part was taking the medicine from Mexico. Severita would not spit out this pill.

One night when everyone was asleep, Severita heard crying and talking in the bedroom next to hers. It was her mother and father. She strained to hear what they were saying. She wanted to know why they were crying. She clearly heard her father sobbing and saying, "Please, God, why are you taking my daughter from us? What has she done to deserve to be crippled like this? Help me understand, God." Severita also began to cry into her pillow. She did not want anyone to know what she had heard. After a few minutes of crying and feeling sorry for herself, her resolve came back. Severita promised herself she would walk again. She promised herself that no matter how much it hurt, she was going to ride that bicycle every day and get well. She was going to go back to school. She told herself she was not ready to die, and continued to force herself to take the medicine.

Springtime came and the Laras started to see the results. The medicine did work. The exercise became less painful and easier for Severita to perform. The massage and manipulation from the chiropractor and her mom was stretching her legs and uncurling her fingers and toes. Dr. Lavasick was good. But Severita was impatient. She cried daily, especially when she lay in bed and through the open window watched her sisters and brother play outside. When her dad would bring her a banana split and the other children only received an ice cream cone, they taunted her with name-calling. They were cruel to her.

The name-calling and taunts only made Severita more determined to walk. And by summer, her toes and fingers had uncurled. She was walking, stiffly and awkwardly, but walking nonetheless. She could hold her fork, knife, and spoon and feed herself. No more help was necessary. She began to dance again.

Her dad had had the foresight to get her daily assignments from Ms. Lanning, the fifth-grade teacher. In fact, he went to the school every day during his lunch hour until the teacher suggested he only come once a week. She even told him not to bother, because Severita would have to repeat the grade. Chemita did not listen. He kept his faith that everything would work out and be all right. He was convinced that Severita would walk again—and begin the sixth grade, come the start of the school year. He continued to bring the latest schoolwork and help Severita with it after he closed the gas station at night. He even convinced the teacher to give him the tests the other students had taken in every subject. Chemita was especially good in math; he could do the computations in his head. Neither Irene nor Chemita had more than a fourth-grade education. Irene learned how to read better in English by helping Severita with her homework, as did Chemita.

When the school year came around, Chemita took Severita to the junior high because she should be in the sixth grade. The principal, Jess Harbin, shook his head and informed him that Severita could not be enrolled in that school; she had to repeat the fifth grade at the grammar school. With his broken English, Mr. Lara made it clear to Mr. Harbin that he had brought home all the schoolwork from all the subjects every day, including the tests, and made Severita do it every night. Mr. Lara pulled out hundreds of pages of graded school work and tests. He began to read the grades out proudly, "One hundred, ninety-three, one hundred, one hundred, ninety, one hundred . . ."

Mr. Harbin stopped him, saying, "That's enough." He could not believe this story. He called the grammar school and asked that Severita's fifth-grade teacher come to his school and help him with this parent-student problem. Ms. Lanning came and did in fact verify that Mr. Lara not only came daily for schoolwork until she told him to come weekly, but also that he returned the completed homework and tests for her to grade. She also added that Severita might know some of the material but the fact that she did not attend school for almost the entire school year made it impossible for her to be passed to the sixth grade. She recommended that Severita redo the fifth grade. Mr. Harbin again told

Mr. Lara to take Severita back to the grammar school and reen-
roll her into the fifth grade with Ms. Lanning.

Mr. Lara did not take no for an answer. Severita had worked
so hard at her schoolwork every night so as to not to be left behind
by her classmates. In his best English, Mr. Lara asked the principal
if attendance was more important than grades. The principal
immediately responded that attendance was important and usually poor attendance meant poor grades, but that grades were the
basis for promotion and therefore most important. With those
words in the air, Mr. Lara threw out a challenge: test Severita.

He said, "You give Severita every test in every subject for as
many days as you want, and if she passes everything, she goes to
sixth grade." The principal was boxed in. He could not wiggle out
of what he had said, and if Severita could handle the material,
she should be in the sixth grade. Mr. Harbin doubted Severita
could pass tests in all subjects, however. It was just too much
material to remember and recall on tests. Mr. Lara insisted that
Severita be given a chance to prove she had done the work and,
more importantly, learned all the material. Together, the three of
them, Mr. Lara, Ms. Lanning, and the principal, agreed on dates
for the tests as Severita listened. The deal was that Ms. Lanning
would put together new tests in all subjects for Severita, and
Severita would take these tests in the few days before the start of
school. If Severita passed all subjects, she would be enrolled in
the sixth grade. If not, she would return to repeat the fifth grade.
It was a done deal as far as Mr. Lara was concerned. He knew his
daughter was smart and could pass all those tests. Severita was
not so sure.

As they drove home, she said, "Daddy, I can't do it. I can't
remember everything. I'm going to fail and have to go back to the
fifth grade. The kids are going to make fun of me."

"Stop, stop, stop," he said in Spanish. "First of all, you will never
again say, 'I can't.' Look at you now. You are walking. You are dancing. You are well again. And all the doctors said to us you would die
or never walk again. You are very strong. If you say you can do

something, you will do it. I believe in you, *mi chiquita*. You are very smart. You are going to pass every test with high grades. No one is going to make fun of you. In fact, everyone is going to ask you, 'How could you do this?'"

Severita listened to his words. She felt bad because her dad was telling her what she felt in her heart. She could pass the tests. She knew she was smart and loved to study. She was just afraid of failure and ridicule.

They drove home in silence after that. With the hot air hitting her face, she began to cry. She also began to recall the sacrifice her dad had made every day and every night to help her with schoolwork. She knew he did not know English that well, but he never complained or quit on her. He kept trying because he believed in her. Severita smiled to herself as she recalled her dad reading out her grades to Mr. Harbin. He was like a lawyer arguing a case, flicking the homework, reading out the grades, waving the papers in the air, and putting Mr. Harbin on the spot with his question about grades and attendance. Her dad was a fighter for her. She remembered her mother who knew even less English; she actually learned more English while reading Nancy Drew mistery novels to her. Her mother was very stern, sometimes Severita thought mean, but her toughness and lack of compromise on exercise got her to walk during the summer. Severita felt she could not let them down.

When they reached home, Severita turned to her dad with dry tear tracks on her cheeks and said, "I will not let you down. You are right. I am smart and I will pass all those tests, no matter how many they give me. I can do it, daddy."

Her father's eyes became watery and he leaned over and hugged his daughter tightly. He was so proud of her.

The day came for the tests and Severita got busy. She had two tests, one in the morning and one in the afternoon. Her father would bring her lunch. At the end of the day, she was shocked to hear Mr. Harbin tell her that testing would continue like this for three more days. But her dad again reassured her on the ride home that if they were as easy as the first two, what did it matter how many days it took? Severita agreed. She was going to go to the sixth grade and be with her friends. That was the goal.

The routine was the same for four days. Severita would get up early and eat breakfast, be driven to school in the cool, early morning air, take two tests with a brief lunch break, then dad would drive her home in the midafternoon, hot summer air, and she would tell her mom about the tests for that day. No word came from Mr. Harbin for five more days after that. On the early morning of school's first day, the junior high secretary called and said Severita has passed every test with very, very good grades. The family was overjoyed, and Mr. Lara announced to all his children that he would take them first and Severita last, because he wanted to see Mr. Harbin's face when they met.

Not only was Mr. Lara very proud that Severita had passed her examinations, but also that he had been able to strike the deal with Mr. Harbin. Now the remaining problem was to get the principal to agree to let Severita take all her classes on the ground floor and not have to walk up stairs or run in the physical education class. Mr. Lara had the doctor's note for the running, but not the stairs issue. When they arrived and went to the principal's office, the first classes had just begun. Mr. Harbin came down the hall and met them by his door. Mr. Lara began to thank him in his usual broken English, but was interrupted by the principal.

"Chemita, before you get to tell me, 'I told you so,' let me assure you that we had all the confidence in the world that Severita would do well. She is a very smart girl. Now, she must run to class. She is late." And turning to Severita, he said, "Get your schedule from my secretary and scoot."

"*No, m'ija, no,*" Mr. Lara instructed Severita, "wait."

He pulled out the doctor's note from his nicely ironed shirt pocket with a Humble gas station patch above it, and said to Mr. Harbin, "My daughter cannot run and she cannot walk up the stairs. Please talk to the secretary to make sure all her classes are downstairs until she can walk up stairs and run."

The principal could not believe his ears. Now this girl was going to get more special privileges. But he knew a doctor's note about a medical condition was more than getting a privilege; it was a right.

Without looking, he told Severita, "Just tell the secretary I said to put this in your file and give you all downstairs classes." And turning to Mr. Lara, he asked, "Anything else, Chemita?" in a sarcastic tone. Without waiting for an answer, Mr. Harbin walked off into his office.

No one read the doctor's note that said, "No running," not the secretary and not the principal. Severita got all her classes downstairs for that fall.

By spring Severita could run and walk up the stairs without help and without someone carrying her books. She continued to earn good grades in all her classes. Her friends did ask her on more than one occasion, "How could you do this? How did Harbin let you?" They all thought Mr. Harbin was really mean and horrible. And he could be, especially when it came to students who spoke Spanish. He prohibited the speaking of Spanish in school, except in Spanish class. The "No Spanish" rule was enforced in the classroom, cafeteria, halls, playground, auditorium, and sidewalks around the school. The rule applied to Chicano students only. Anglo students did not speak Spanish, even if they could a little bit. If a student spoke Spanish and was caught or reported by another student, the matter was handled by Mr. Harbin. The boys got a choice of three days suspension from school or three hits on their butt with his special paddle. The special paddle was a shaved baseball bat with large holes to let air pass through as he swung it to hit the student. Mr. Harbin could hit very hard. After three licks with the special paddle, your bottom was sore and bruised for days. Mr. Harbin handled the girls differently. This was a time when the fashion was big skirts made fuller with lots of petticoats underneath. Mr. Harbin would lift the girls skirt and petticoats with one hand, until he got to the panties, and then hit them. The boys got hit with the special paddle on their bottoms but over the pants, usually jeans, sometimes khakis. Mr. Harbin used both hands to swing the paddle with the boys but only one hand with the girls.

Severita was caught speaking Spanish in the eighth grade and was immediately sent to Mr. Harbin's office. As soon as she walked in and without warning, he ordered her to turn around, lean forward and hold on to the edge of his desk. He lifted her skirt, petticoats and all. He held her down with his elbow on the small of her back, and proceeded to give her three hits on her almost bare bottom. Severita cried out in severe pain with the first hit. The paddling made her legs hurt, like when she was sick. But she could not break way from him. He hit her again and again. Severita could barely see because of the tears in her eyes and could not hear because of the pain all over her body. She ran out of the office and into the street. As best she could, with some running, some walking, some jogging, she made it to her dad's gas station, a distance of about twenty-two blocks. Still crying, she told him what had happened. Mr. Lara's face turned ashen. He could not believe what he was hearing. Dropping the tire tools he had in his hand, he yelled to another employee to care for the station, and proceeded to the school with Severita. He was speeding and parked illegally right in front of the school. "Come on!" he commanded Severita to follow.

Chemita did not wait for the secretary to announce his arrival. He barged in on Mr. Harbin and went straight to him, walking around the desk, pointing his finger in his face. "You not hit my daughter. You not hit my sick daughter. You not hit for Spanish. Spanish is mine. My language. You English. Me Spanish. My daughter also Spanish. My culture."

Severita was afraid for her dad. The principal was a larger man and younger. Mr. Harbin was now standing and trying to get Mr. Lara to back up. Instead of backing up, Mr. Lara grabbed the principal by the front of his shirt, tie and all, and began banging him on the wall, still yelling at him. "You no hit my sick daughter. You English. Me Spanish. You stupid rule."

The secretary came in screaming at Mr. Lara, "Let him go. I'm going to call the police."

Severita began screaming, "No, daddy, no. They will call the police. Leave him alone. No, daddy, no."

To his credit, Mr. Harbin remained as calm as he could under the circumstances and kept saying, "Chemita, calm down. Let's talk about this. I'm sorry. Chemita, calm down."

And since Mr. Harbin was not fighting back, Chemita did calm down and let him go. The principal told his secretary to just go outside and not call anyone. He tried to explain his "No Spanish" rule to Chemita.

When the principal said it was to make students learn English, Chemita countered with, "She know English as good as you."

When he said it was to Americanize the Mexican children, Chemita said, "She born American, no need your help."

When he said it was to make the students more proficient in English, Chemita said, "Two languages make you twice as good."

When the principal ran out of arguments, Chemita began his tirade again about Spanish being his language and, therefore, Severita's, that he wanted her to keep her Spanish, that she could speak both, and, that Harbin could keep his English but not take her Spanish.

And, working himself up all over again, "You no hit my daughter. Never!"

Mr. Harbin finally said, "Okay Chemita, I will never spank her. But she can't speak Spanish in school."

The incident stayed like that without clear resolution, but the story circulated all over the school and throughout the community. Mr. Harbin continued to gas up his car at the Lara's gas station on credit. He and Chemita did not talk as much to each other as before. Mr. Harbin really knew now that Chemita would stand up and do anything for his children. Severita continued to speak Spanish anywhere she wanted in school. Only one teacher kept reporting her, and when that happened, Mr. Harbin's secretary just sent Severita to the library. Severita loved that punishment because she could read more Nancy Drew mysteries. Again, her friends would ask her, "How can you do this? Did your dad really beat up Harbin?"

Severita completed her junior high years with her classmates. She made really good grades and graduated to high school. She looked forward to that new experience. As the school term ended, Severita and Linda discussed how to approach their parents about going up north for the seasonal agricultural work like almost every one of their relatives and school friends. They wanted to be migrants, like every other Chicano in Crystal City.

Chapter 3
The Trek Up North

The summer of 1968 was rapidly approaching, and Severita and Linda did not want to spend another suffocating summer in Crystal City. It was so, so hot. The ground burned as if on fire. At night, the open windows made no difference. There was no air moving. The bed was hot and the sweat from their bodies made it insufferable. Each pair of sisters shared a bed, as did the boys in another room. Each of them hated to touch the other's sweaty skin as they tossed and turned. It was like living in an oven day and night, breathing hot air and walking around sweaty and sticky from the humidity. And they still had an outhouse in the back. Going out at night to the outhouse was dangerous because all the animals, snakes included, became nocturnal in the heat of the summer and were out and about. They sleep during the day.

Severita and Linda were teenagers now, young women. Their mother had never explained menstruation to them, but María Saucedo, a neighbor, did to Severita. She in turn explained it to Linda, and the two of them added feminine hygiene products to the weekly grocery list that they and their dad were responsible for.

María Serna, another neighbor, invited them to go north with her family that coming summer. María was divorced from Victoriano Serna, but had three older sons very loyal to her: Víctor, Rubén, and Ramiro. Each was married with children and lived in their houses, but they trekked up north together to help their mother earn summer income to make it during the winter. There were few jobs for Mexicans in Crystal City, and even fewer for unskilled women. The major source of employment was the Del

Monte Packing Corporation that canned vegetables and juices. The plant offered about 800 jobs during peak season to women packers and canners. María Serna discussed her idea with Chemita and Irene passed on the invitation to the girls. She assured the parents that the girls would be no bother or extra load on anyone.

Severita and Linda's friends continued to talk about how much fun they had up north and how great it was to make their own money for clothes and other expenses. Chemita always bought the girls things they wanted and gave them spending money. He had even allowed Severita to sign up in a Hollywood magazine to be the local sales representative for cosmetics. Severita lied about her age to the company and lied to her parents as to her motive. She wanted to wear makeup, which with her parents was next to impossible until she married. Her mother did not wear any makeup, much less lipstick. When asked why, she would answer that to a decent woman, that was evil. The Lara girls noticed that their mother never allowed their father to kiss her on the lips, only her cheeks.

As the exclusive sales representative for Studio Girl in Crystal City, Severita made real money. She showed the older girls and women the ad in a Hollywood magazine and demonstrated the products. She explained to her mother that a salesperson had to model the product for her customers. If she did not use them, then why should her customers buy them? She sold cosmetics at school undercover. She sold cosmetics to women in cars while her dad pumped gasoline at the station. She took samples over to the barmaids at both of her dad's cantinas. He now owned La Perla next door and La Victoria by Canela's Bakery and Suse's school. For two years Severita sold cosmetics and earned extra money, but she still wanted to go up north and be a migrant laborer.

Together, Severita, Linda, and María Serna ganged up on Chemita, insisting he let them go up north. Mr. Lara knew better than to engage in argument with Severita or Linda in front of María Serna. He knew she was a good woman, and her grown sons were very respectful and hardworking, but he also knew how hard agricultural work was. He promised to think it over and he did. Several times during the remaining days, the girls came up with novel arguments such as wanting to work to save money in order to go visit Uncles Nicolás and Bruno, his brothers in California, the following summer. Severita even tried explaining she needed to go to Hollywood to meet her employer, Studio Girl Cosmetics, in order to discuss with them why her sales commissions had not increased.

Chemita had only one argument against the idea of going up north in search of agricultural work. It was simply too hard. The girls were not in shape or used to such hard manual labor from early morning to late evening. He told them and told them. The advice went in one ear and out the other.

Irene *did* want the girls to go; the experience would teach them the value of money and expose them to really hard work. It was work she knew how to perform as a young teenager in her sharecropper family. And she would have less housework with two of them gone during the summer.

Chemita agreed to let them go, with various conditions: if they went, they could not come back for any reason. Except for dire illness, they had to work all summer until the Sernas came back. And they could not stay home, sleep late, and pretend to be sick or hurting from soreness while the others worked in the fields. Severita and Linda had to agree to pay María Serna their share of expenses from the money earned by the two of them before they bought anything with the money they would earn.

Chemita looked at both his girls in their eyes, first one then the other, "I am not sending you money to come back before the summer ends. I am not letting María Serna send you back. If you go with the Sernas you return with the Sernas. And you will not call home collect every time you are homesick or sore. You will call once a month after payday with your money to tell me you paid your bills to María and saved the rest for the trip home."

Chemita knew the girls were about to undergo an ordeal never to be forgotten in their lives, but he knew they had to begin making decisions on their own. This hard work surely would make them want to go to college and stay out of tending crops for others at cheap wages. He wanted his girls to be independent and educated, to never depend on a man for survival.

"A woman always keeps the kids and has to be responsible for the lives of others," he frequently told them. "Men are not responsible, they just walk away."

For days prior to the trip, the oldest son, Víctor, came around to remind the girls not take too much with them, only work clothes and warm clothing, because Minnesota, where they were going, was still cold and sometimes rainy into mid-July. Within days of final exams, the girls packed their things into one borrowed cardboard suitcase.

Víctor laughed when he saw the Studio Girl cosmetic case and said, "You will not need that for yourself or have time to sell to others. Leave it."

Severita began to rethink the situation. Maybe this was not such a good idea, but it was too late—the truck was already boarding. It was a double ton-and-a-half vehicle with wooden sides going up about four feet and was covered with a thick tarpaulin from the cab to end of bed—about fifteen feet. Inside that makeshift canvas shelter were six families with children. Severita and Linda were advised to sit together toward the cab area and to avoid the back door because it was too cold and noisy there.

The Lara girls hugged their mom and dad tightly and said, "*Adiós.* We'll be back with lots of money, you'll see."

As they climbed up the wobbly wooden ladder leading to the truck bed, they waved and then disappeared into the dark recesses. The hot Texas sun was still high on the horizon, but it was about 6 p.m. Linda grabbed Severita's hand and placed it on her heart. It was beating so fast.

She said, "We're finally going north. I can't wait to get there."

Severita concurred, "Me too. I wish we were already there and working."

The huge truck noisily creaked its way into a turn and made it over the tracks, swaying from side to side. It was loaded down. The Lara girls could only see backwards—out the rear end that was kept open for air. That was the only air for the bed passengers. When they made the turn onto North First Street, they saw their dad's gas station. Severita and Linda knew Highway 83 would be the connection just a few blocks away. Highway 83 would take them all the way to Minnesota—no need to turn anywhere. Once they hit the highway and the gears ran out, the truck hit top speed.

The girls realized how really hot and suffocating it was in the rear. There was no fresh air, not even hot fresh air. The noise of the truck made them sleepy, but the stench of sweat and other smells made them nauseated. There was also the pervasive smell of gas fumes. Linda felt like throwing up more than once, but Severita made her suck on a lemon their mother had packed with their snack food. She had also packed Vick's Vapor Rub for their chests and the soles of feet in cold weather and *té de manzanilla*, chamomile tea, for upset stomachs. But on the truck, Linda could not drink water or tea; otherwise she would need to go to the bathroom. At the frequent stops for gas and food, the men in the rear would jump out quickly for a smoke and bodily needs. The women and girls used a can to relieve themselves inside the truck bed. Everyone was crowded in and could not stand up for lack of room.

The big truck lumbered as it geared up for speed. The rear passengers felt as if they were riding a big halting monster that made their heads snap back and forth. The gears made noise and took many shifts before they hit a top speed of forty to fifty miles per hour, with the heavy load of people on board.

By the first morning, the girls had eaten all of their snacks and finished their little jug of water. Everyone looked disheveled. No shower nor bath nor running hot water was available on the truck for morning cleanup. There was no bathroom either, just the tin can. When the dawn light filtered inside the back of the truck, the women had to hold up a sheet or blanket to surround the user of the tin can. When they stopped on the road the next morning, it was still hot. They were still in Texas, near Fort Worth. The Lara girls began to realize how large Texas really was, and how many more days of travel in that smelly back bed they would have to endure. They also realized that Mexicans were not wanted in restaurants, bathrooms at gas stations, or at parks. They simply were refused service. Severita and Linda had seen and experienced discrimination in Crystal City, beginning at school, but not this blatant. Usually Víctor, the largest man of them all at 6 feet 6 inches, would go inside a restaurant or store and place an order, then walk to the back side of the building to pay and get the food. Everyone else waited by the truck, enjoying what hot fresh air they could gasp. Sometimes, before gassing up the large truck, Víctor would ask the attendant if all of them could use the bathrooms. Sometimes it worked, sometimes it didn't.

The most accommodating place was a roadside park where the women and sometimes the men would grill meat over an open fire. Everyone could run and jump and scream and holler to his heart's content. In the truck, where everyone held his spot by laying on it, they spoke in muffled tones and just stared into the darkness or the bits of light that filtered through the cracks, creases, and holes in the tarp. The dread was the feeling of having a bowel movement and not being able to hold it to the next stop.

The truck made its way across Oklahoma that next day and to the edge of Kansas. They had stopped several times during the day, and not for gas; something was wrong, but no one would ask the drivers. By late afternoon, they hit a thunderstorm, and the truck edged to the side of the road because visibility was very poor. It was raining so much and the wind blowing so hard that the truck rocked and trembled. Everyone was trying to see out the little back door and also gasp the strange frigid air that whipped into the bed of the truck. The rain made a horribly loud noise against the tarp. The space between the people and the canvass top was only a foot or two at most. To Severita and Linda it was as if the noise itself was hitting them. Then it began. The noise from the rain began to change in tone; it was as if the raindrops were being tossed against the canvas harder and the noise was getting louder and louder.

Suddenly, the truck doors slammed up front and Rubén and Ramiro Serna were standing by the back door yelling for some blankets to cover the windshield. It was hail coming down, marble size. They wanted blankets to cover the glass and keep it from shattering from the hail if it got larger. No sooner than the blankets were tossed, the hail got larger. The people in back could hear the screams of pain from both Serna brothers being pelted by the larger hail as they grappled with the blankets in the wind, trying to tie them down to protect the windshield. The people in back could see the ground covered with what looked like mothballs. The Lara girls had not seen hail as large as golf balls in their lives.

Then it got very dark and scary. The wind was so ferocious that the truck seemed to rise and fall. The noise was deafening. Some of the women and children began to scream with fear. Severita and Linda hugged one another tightly and began to cry. One of the men in back yelled out, "It's a tornado! Close the door! Quick!" The Lara sisters knew what a tornado was. They just had not seen one, much less been targeted by one.

As suddenly as the storm had come, it disappeared. The roar of the wind seemed to travel down the road, leaving them behind in cold eerie silence. No sound, just a distant and fading roar. The sunlight came back. Again, the Serna brothers appeared at the back door, banging for someone to open it and come out. As soon as the back door was opened, the people in back got down, stepping into the cold air and layers of frozen hail balls. Severita and Linda, along with the other children, gathered frozen balls of hail and tasted them. They had been through a tornado. They had been scared, but now it was fun.

The next major stop was somewhere in Kansas, where the truck broke down during the night. The part to fix it would not be available until the next day. The talk among those in the back centered on the tornado of the evening before and on when the truck would be fixed. The good thing about the stop was that it was near the edge of a town, and a Mexican family lived in a nearby farm-house. The man from the house came over and invited the women and children to visit his home and his family. They had been migrants ten years earlier and decided to settle there because work was plentiful. The women in the truck were ecstatic because they got to wash up and walk around the farmhouse. They spent time visiting with the woman and each other instead of just sitting in the cramped truck bed. They got to drink homemade coffee. The kids chased chickens, played with the dogs, and ate warm tortillas made fresh by the lady of the house.

The truck was finally fixed and back on the road, but they had lost several hours of travel time and spent more money on the repair because the mechanic had to come out to fix it. The mechanic had also told them that an inside rear tire on the left was flat and they should fix it now or have to stop for a longer time later. The Sernas wanted to get going and decided to chance it because the other tire was still good. Had they known about the flat tire when they waited for the part or when the mechanic was fixing the truck, the tire would have been fixed. As they traveled up Highway 83, the weather got colder. At first everyone thought it was the leftover cold from the tornado, but now it seemed it was just colder in Kansas and even more so by the time they got to Nebraska the next morning. Severita and Linda had a chance to sit by the back door and look out, but had to wrap a blanket around themselves because it was cold.

No sooner had the truck crossed the Platte River than a tire blew. Fortunately, it was not the tire next to the one that was already flat. Unfortunately, it was too much of a gamble to keep traveling on two flat tires and only two remaining good ones. Besides, the truck had a spare. But in the changing of the tire, they lost more time. Everyone had to get out of the truck to lighten the load and watch the men labor with the giant tires. Without a spare now, the Sernas decided to stop in the next town and get both tires repaired. The repairs took more time and meant more money spent. María told the girls that any other repair would be difficult because they had exhausted the money and had only enough for gasoline. The truck moved on into South Dakota. They now had been on the road for three days and still had North Dakota to cross before reaching Minnesota. Shelly, their destination in Minnesota, was not far from the border with North Dakota.

When they arrived at the farmer's house in Shelly, it was past midnight of the fourth night. Víctor went to the back door and announced their arrival, but asked everyone to stay inside the truck for the night until they could talk to the grower. They had his name and address, but had not fully negotiated the terms of the summer contract with him nor arranged for housing. The girls could not go back to sleep and tossed and turned until dawn. When they finally got down from the truck and saw the farmland, they were shocked. First of all, it was cold and foggy. The ground was wet and muddy. Secondly, the farmhouse was large and had a basement. A large red barn was down the road about half a block away. A smaller red building sat opposite the barn with trac- tors, tanks, pull wagons, and other farm implements scattered everywhere. Lastly, surrounding these buildings were rows and rows of some crop they would work on, but they did not recog- nize the sugar beets they would soon be picking. When they asked María about the rows, she told them each was a mile long and that each of them would do about thirty to forty rows. Linda and Severita did not know what that meant, but soon would find out.

The farmer sent them down the road to a small clearing next to a stand of tall trees, where four shacks faced each other. Some of the people in the truck got down with their belongings at this location. Others were dropped off at another location with simi- lar surroundings. María, with her sons, their wives, and children as well as Severita and Linda, got down at a place almost identi- cal to the first. Their new home was a shack. Each son and family had a shack to themselves. Severita and Linda shared their shack with María and her three other children, six in all. The shack had three rooms, a kitchen and two bedrooms, all very small. There was only one door to the house, in the front. The walls had no insulation and it was all very, very dirty. The metal beds inside had horrible, smelly mattresses, stained and torn. The kitchen had a four-burner stove, a sink, and a wooden table with two benches. A single light bulb hung in the center of each room. There were no closets, just nails on the wall studs to hang clothes, towels, or coats. At the front door, was a hanging mirror, cracked and stained at the edges. Severita and Linda got one of the beds to share and under advice from María, covered the mattress with cardboard from the boxes she brought with dishes, pots and pans, clothes, towels, linen, and blankets. María lent the girls a set of sheets and one blanket. They had brought a towel and a blanket each, but no sheets or pillows, much less pillowcases. The toilet, like at home, was outside. Water, unlike home, was also outside, only drawn from a hand pump. The water was always ice-cold.

The first nights in the shack were a nightmare. The cardboard on the mattresses made noise whenever anyone moved. The cold and wind seemed to find every crack and hole in the wall to come through. Giant rats also shared the shack and would come out nightly. The rats would drop from the rafters and scurry over the girls as they slept. After screaming and yelling and jumping out of bed several times during the first night, the girls learned to sleep all covered up from head to toe.

If the first nights were nightmares, the first days on the farm were daymares. The fields were too wet to work so they had to stay home and wait for the land to dry. There was nowhere to go and nothing to do except sit in the shack, play in the stand of trees, walk on the road avoiding the mud and puddles, and go to the outdoor toilet. The outhouse was creepy. It had only one hole, not two like the Laras' privy. It did not sit straight on the ground, but crooked as if it were about to fall or had fallen and had been picked up again. It smelled really, really bad. Worst of all, the graffiti on the outhouse walls, inside and out, read: "Get out of here! Racist Gringo! Bay pay, bad man!" Because the Sernas had never worked this farm before, they had no clue as to what these warnings meant.

After two more days of waiting, María told Víctor to go check on the other families and go into town to buy groceries. They had no food, only the staples of flour, spices, some beans and potatoes. She needed lard, red pepper, serrano peppers, onions, garlic, ground pork, and more beans and potatoes. The girls wanted to go, and María let them. It was fun riding in the back of the big truck without the mounds of their things, and all the people. They both sat at the back door dangling their legs as they inspected Shelly, Minnesota. Shelly was not a large city—they were disappointed. There was no mall, only one grocery store, one theater, one church, not Catholic, and two gas stations, one with a washateria next to it. They had yet to see anything resembling the mall their friends had told them about. Shelly people stared at them as if they were unwanted foreigners; some made faces. Most of the grown white men wore the blue jean overalls, characteristic of farmers. Perhaps they were farmers, walking around town also waiting for the land to dry.

Work finally came. María announced to all in the shacks that the next morning she would have the tortillas ready for everybody to make their lunches to take to the fields. She told everyone to go to sleep early because tomorrow and the next few days would be the longest days of their lives. Severita and Linda looked at each other trying to figure out this riddle. Why longest?

The smell of coffee boiling and *chorizo* sizzling woke the girls up along with the others in the shack. But it was dark. María had a basin of hot water ready for the first ones up to use for washing up. She told the girls to pick out their worst work clothes to wear and to wear them until they were ready to be thrown away. "Work clothes were not to be washed but worn out," she said.

That first work morning María asked Linda to get another bucket of water from the hand pump outside. Linda came back with her eyes wide open and watery, her lips purple, and goose bumps all over her arms.

As she struggled with a half pail of water, she said, "It's freezing outside. I couldn't feel my fingers anymore."

Severita asked, "We are going to work out there in the dark when it is freezing?"

"*Sí,*" María answered without even turning to look at her and continuing to flip two tortillas on the long *comal*. María was an expert cook. She could make her own *chorizo* and had to, because the store in Shelly, as in other places, did not have Mexican food products. She could make eight dozen tortillas in about an hour, start to finish. She made a small mountain of tortillas every morning, Saturday and Sunday included, for her sons and wives and children, and the Lara girls. The morning tortillas had to last the day. Tortillas were consumed for breakfast, two or three each, and two or three more for the noon meal out in the fields. Sometimes the grown men consumed four or five at each meal. What tortillas were left were for dinner. The wives of her sons could make tortillas, but not as good as María's. María did not cook anything else for all the other families, only for those living with her in her shack.

When they got to the field, María and Víctor took time to teach Severita and Linda how to work the beet row. They explained that the summer work consisted of three phases on the same rows. First, they would walk along the row and cut out the beet seedlings with a whack of the long-handled hoe. The idea was to thin the plants so the remaining ones could grow big and healthy. It would take them about two weeks to do their 200 rows, all of them working together as a crew. The next phase was weeding. As the sugar beet plants grew, so would the weeds next to them. The weeds, not the sugar beet, had to be cut out, again with the hoe or by hand. The girls were warned: "If you don't cut out the weeds, you will suffer the consequences when we have to harvest the beets." Sometimes it took two or three weedings to grow sugar beets big enough. Finally, the harvest would be done by machine or hand, depending on what equipment the farmer had. The migrant crew would be paid by the work done on the entire field.

The farmer paid one price for thinning, another for weeding, and another for harvesting, and more if the Serna truck was used for hauling the crop to the sugar mill. The Lara girls finally learned that in the United States sugar came from sugar beets, not from sugarcane as in Mexico and the Caribbean.

When the rows were assigned to each by María, the crew took off. It was still dark and the tiny plants were hard to see. Severita and Linda were nervous about cutting too many or not cutting enough with every whack of their hoes. The fun lasted about twenty minutes. By then, the girls could hear others but not see them. The bottoms of their pants were wet and their socks and shoes soaked. Their feet felt heavy because they were sopping with mud and water. By the time the sun came out clearly, Víctor, Rubén, Ramiro, and María were little figures in the distance. They were experienced workers and moved quickly and efficiently. The faster acres were done, the more money they made. Between the girls, who were last, and the men with María in front, were the wives and other grown children. Their small babies were left in the truck alone. Other families left their babies in cars. By a half mile down in any row, you could neither see the ends of the row nor the truck or cars.

The girls felt overwhelmed, as if they could not finish one row, much less the thirty or forty they signed up to do over the summer. The rows at one mile each were just too long. By midmorning their arms felt like their legs: deadweight. The hoe seemed to weigh more and more with each stroke. Severita and Linda had never worked like this before.

At lunchtime when everyone was digging into their bags for the *tacos* filled with *chorizo* and *frijoles*, María told the girls to go behind the truck to pee or to take some toilet paper and do it between the rows. She just said it as if it were no big deal. And it was no big deal because everyone was too busy looking at the plants in the row for a precise whack of the hoe to notice who was behind them or stopping. The tree lines that separated these monstrously large fields were also miles away. It was crazy to walk all the way to the trees and back just to pee. Severita and Linda both learned to pee in between the rows.

The girls made it through the day. Everyone was proud of each other for having done four rows each. Of course, the grown men and María did most of that, sometimes circling back to help a younger member of the crew, including Severita and Linda. By the time they got home, the girls and a few others were dozing off. Neither Severita nor Linda wanted supper; they were exhausted. All they wanted was sleep and even bypassed washing up. That night, neither one undressed or covered up, and they forgot about the rats.

Before too long, María was shaking them to get up and get ready for work. The food was on the table and their lunches were packed.

But they could not move. They heard María. They could see her face in the near darkness, but could not move an arm or a leg. They were paralyzed from soreness and hurt.

Linda called out to Severita in panic, "I can't move my arm, it hurts so much! ¡Ay!"

Severita had flashbacks to her terrible illness. She could not move either. They struggled to rise and put their muddy shoes on. Severita and Linda stumbled into the light of the kitchen area and saw that the others were in similar shape, with hurt in their eyes. No one at the table had combed his hair or washed his face. They could not raise their arms. The hot water kettle remained full on the stove.

María laughed and said, "It only hurts the first few days, and then you will be in shape." She moved from person to person giving them a rubdown that did not help, but made each one discover new body areas of pain.

The second day was like the first day, never-ending and even more painful. By lunchtime the hurt and pain from the day before seemed to subside, only to be replaced by new aches and pain by late afternoon. But it was still a beautiful day, and María polled the crew to see if they wanted to go an extra hour. No one wanted to except for her grown sons.

María announced to everyone, "We came to work. Yes, you hurt, but hurt only goes away with more work. We were late in starting because of the rain. We lost days. Tomorrow we stay an extra hour, no voting."

María was in charge. Despite her three grown sons being ex-Navy servicemen and having families of their own, she made the decisions for all and kept the crew on task.

Each day seemed like an eternity to Severita and Linda. They hurt in every part of their body. Both believed they would die in the fields and actually wished it to happen, rather than call their dad to send money for them to come home. Every day was just like the one before it. There was no television, radio, movies, reading, going for a Coke—nothing but work, sleep, work. On the first weekend, which really was only Sunday off, they went into Shelly, but only to wash clothes and buy groceries. There was no time for a movie. They had to come back and hang clothes to dry and change the sheets on the beds. Severita and Linda chose to throw away the socks, panties, and pants they wore that week rather than wash them. Sunday morning, they all took turns pumping water and heating it for bathing, one by one, in the kitchen. The big wash tubs they had brought came in handy for that, as well as to wash clothes between trips to Shelly.

That Sunday, the girls got change made from their last dollars and called their dad from the pay phone in the laundromat. María had told them not to, but they did not listen. Chemita answered the phone. Just seconds into the greetings and pleasantries of how much they missed each other and what an experience the trip was, the girls started crying and pleading with their dad to send money so they could go home.

Severita tried psychology on him: "You were so right, daddy, like you always are. We were wrong. We want to come home."

Linda mostly just cried when she had the phone. "I can't brush my hair. I can't put on my shoes. I'm dirty all the time. I don't want to do this anymore."

But Chemita, even while hurting inside, only offered tough love: "No. I warned you. You return when the work is done."

On the next trip into town, the girls called again, and their dad said the same thing. He also thanked them for not calling collect, because he would not have accepted their call if they had. Thank goodness he had warned them, because they had no more money. All the money they brought was spent on Cokes, candy, Hollywood magazines, and snacks during the visits to Shelly. Faced with their dad's closed door and the fact that María's prediction of hurting less the more they worked was coming true, the work routine became that, a routine. The only difference now was the longer days. The sun stayed up in the sky until really late. Work now began at 5:30 in the morning and ended around 9 at night.

The cold dawns became cool mornings and hot days. The sun burned them as much as the Texas sun, and the entire crew was soon wearing long-sleeved shirts and hats for protection from the relentless sun. One morning, not unusual in any way, the crew got into their rows and began another dragged-out, horrible workday. By midmorning, the girls were way behind all of the others. They were now weeding, but the job they had done at thinning was not the best, so they had to thin and weed at the same time. Suddenly, Linda started crying. She was sitting in the middle of the row bawling like a baby, when Severita looked back to see what was wrong. Linda would not answer her, just wailed louder with every question, "What happened, Linda? Did something bite you? Are you hurt? What happened?" No answer, just loud crying.

In desperation Severita looked around for help and could not see anyone. She removed Linda's hat, stroked her hair, wiped the tears from her face and held her tightly,

"What's the matter? Does your stomach ache?"

Nothing. But at least Linda reached around and hugged Severita back, sobbing even louder. Now she was shaking uncontrollably with every gasp of air between sobs.

Finally, Linda said something Severita could not understand. It sounded foreign—maybe it was English.

"Say again," Severita told her.

"Nobody remembered me. Nobody loves me. It's my birthday, and here I am in this field with no one around but you. And you forgot my birthday."

It was Linda's birthday. Here she was, out in the beet fields of the Red River Valley in Minnesota, more than a thousand miles from home and without a happy moment the entire summer.

Both sisters began to cry—Linda because life was not fair, Severita because Linda was crying. Linda had made her feel bad for forgetting her birthday. At home, there may not have been elaborate birthday parties with piñatas and gifts, but none was ever forgotten.

As the girls continued to cry loudly, María and Víctor ran between the rows to come to their aid. "What's the matter? What happened?"

Between sobs and shakes, Severita explained the crisis of the forgotten birthday. Víctor shrugged, huffed, and stormed back to his work. María gently rubbed Linda and Severita on the nape of the neck and urged them to get up and return to work. She promised to make something special for Linda that night.

María found a Hershey chocolate bar in the cupboard of the shack. She mashed it with milk and made hot chocolate for all of the family members. Everyone had brought Linda something: a magazine, ribbons for her hair, nail polish, and a handful of wild flowers. Severita led the singing of "Happy Birthday." Linda would never forget the horrible but wonderful birthday she had near Shelly, Minnesota. She was now fifteen years old and would never have a *quinceañera* party.

Days became weeks and weeks became months. Sometimes it rained, and that was bad because they had nothing to do and more work to catch up on when it dried. When it did rain, the grown men would go into town, sometimes with their wives, and Severita and Linda got to baby-sit their children for extra money. One time it did rain while they were mid-mile of their row. The rain turned into hail, and the workers ran in a panic. They could see a funnel cloud in the distance. Víctor and Rubén ran toward them, yelling to run to the truck. The tornado was very, very near.

They made it to the truck and headed for their shacks, but the tornado was coming straight at them. Víctor made a U-turn in the road and headed for the farmer's home to get into the basement. Everyone was screaming at Víctor to go faster, because they could see the tornado gaining on them. The fury of the hail with rain and frigid air, plus the roar of the blasting wind, reminded them of the Kansas tornado. They made it to the farmer's house and they all jumped out while Víctor banged on his door. The wife answered and refused them entry to the basement. She simply said, "No. Use the barn."

The group, drenched in water and pelted by hail, ran down and across the road into the barn. The tornado approached, it roaring like a train. As the group huddled in a corner in what used to be stalls for cows or horses, the roof of the barn was torn off. María was praying in Spanish with a rosary clutched in her hands. Linda was crying uncontrollably. Víctor and the other brothers placed their large bodies over their wives and children as if they could prevent the tornado from sucking them all up along with the roof. Severita was almost in shock at the events as they were unfolding before her eyes. She hugged Linda to comfort her. "Don't worry, little sister, it'll be over soon. Nothing will happen to us."

After the storm passed they hurried home, to see if their shacks were standing, and they were. María called a family meeting that night and announced that the signs referring to their farmer in the outdoor toilet were true. They had to leave immediately. He was a bad man, and so was his wife. It took another week for them to collect from the farmer. He wanted to cheat them out of the number of acres, out of amounts per acre per job, and the total. María had experienced this unfair dealing before. The farmers knew that Mexicans had no local persons to help them fight nor could they hire a lawyer to sue in court, assuming they could stay for the court case. Thus, some farmers cheated them, telling them to take it or leave it. María restrained her sons from any drastic actions against the man or his wife. She persisted in the negotiations and called on an arbitrator from the Farm Bureau to come settle accounts. Finally, they got paid most of what they thought they were entitled to and left for Crookston, South Dakota, to work on another farm.

Crookston had a mall. They saw youngsters skating on ice, a first for the girls from Crystal City. Crookston had a McDonald's, the first ever seen by Severita and Linda. They went to the movies for the first time all summer long. María also had paid the girls their share of the money, $1,000. But with expenses deducted, they had $500 left. Someone had a camera, and the girls took a picture flashing the money. They were so proud of themselves for having stuck it out and earned those hundred dollar bills. Linda asked innocently how María had arrived at that $500 figure for expenses from the $1,000. If she had divided the total by persons in the shack and included her youngest son, Gilberto, the girls should get more. María simply said, "He is a baby and doesn't eat as much." Severita and Linda both laughed because little ten-year-old Gilberto ate more than either one of them and María. But they were so grateful to María for the experience and all she had done for them, cooking, preparing lunches, ironing, washing, cleaning, and helping out in the field.

The job was done in Shelly and the girls did not want to stay in Crookston, so they decided to take a bus home. Before the trip back with their money, they went to the mall and bought themselves some clothes, gifts for the sisters and little brother back home, and something for their parents.

The migrant experience was behind them forever. Their father had been right: it was not for them. They were going to finish high school and go on to college. Their father would always tell them that the best inheritance he could ever give them was an education. The girls learned that a woman could do anything a man could.

Chapter 4
The 1969 Walkout

The following summer, 1969, with money saved from the migrant experience, Severita and Linda again hit the migrant trail, but as tourists. They went to Gilroy, California. A young couple, Apolonio and María del Refugio Moncada, were going there, and the Lara girls hitched a ride. Pole and Cuqui, as the couple was known around town, were very popular. Cuqui had been a cheerleader and Pole a good baseball player. The trip only took two days in an air-conditioned car, which traveled at maximum speeds. The trip was a world of difference from their last. They sat comfortably, ate in good restaurants, relieved themselves in gas station bathrooms, wore sunglasses and shorts. They were tourists, not migrants. What a difference appearance made. All four of them had been migrants at one time or another; none of them had ever been tourists. None of them had been to California.

To pass the time on the road, the four of them talked about everything under the sun, stars, and moon, which they saw plenty of this time. They asked Cuqui about being a cheerleader. Linda wanted to be a cheerleader. Linda had been plump as a child, but now she had developed into a tall and well-figured young teenager. Severita asked Pole and Cuqui about the geometry course with a teacher named Temple Ray, and about Mrs. Lunz, the English teacher. "Is *la* Lunz as bad as Ms. Harper?" Severita inquired. Ms. Harper would instruct Chicano students to sit in the back of the class and not interrupt her. When angry, she would call the Chicano kids's names and often would ask out loud why the school board even allowed them in school. Cuqui assured Severita that Ms. Lunz would be very hard on her but not call her names.

"She probably feels the same way as Ms. Harper, but she won't say it that way. She'll just tell you to go into home economics and to take typing, and that you will never make it in college," Cuqui said.

Pole had quit school because of the way Anglo teachers treated Chicanos. He did not feel welcome in the classrooms, only on the baseball field.

Pole asked Cuqui to tell the Lara girls about the incident that happened during the Popeye Baseball Tournament toward the end of the school year in April 1969. Popeye was the cartoon character, and a statue of his likeness sat in front of city hall, because the city proclaimed itself the Spinach Capital of the World, given the large amount of spinach harvested in the area and processed in the local Del Monte plant. Cuqui obliged.

The incident centered on the Chicano students protesting that the tournament sweetheart was not voted on by students or players of the team. And, as usual, the tournament sweetheart was an Anglo. Chicano students grew more vocal in their protest at the obvious denial of their right to vote for their student favorites in this type of election and the obvious discrimination against Chicanas. In response, the high school principal, John B. Lair, said it was a decision made by the baseball coach and out of his hands. Chicano students demanded a fair election with stated rules of eligibility or no sweetheart be presented at the conclusion of the tournament. Some of the more informed Chicanos began talking about contacting MAYO, a group of militant Chicano youth based in San Antonio. MAYO stood for the Mexican American Youth Organization. MAYO had gained a reputation for fighting for civil rights and educational reform. It had been involved with many school walkouts in the state.

The Lara girls listened attentively to this explanation and Linda asked, "What is a walkout?"

Pole said he did not know for sure, but that he heard it was when Chicano students in protest did not go to school. Cuqui added that it had to do with the money the state of Texas sent to the school districts for student attendance, so when the students did not go to classes, the school district lost money every day.

One of the MAYO members was from Crystal City. He had graduated a few years back. Pole knew him because he had played Little League baseball with him. Another friend from Carrizo Springs, a town just twelve miles south on Highway 83, was also a leader in MAYO. Some of the students, Cuqui did not know who exactly, had called them to come to a meeting about this problem. Severita asked who they were.

Pole said, "José Angel Gutiérrez, Dr. Gutiérrez's son. The other is a Patlán, or some name like that. Didn't your family know Dr. Gutiérrez?"

Severita said that she did not know José Angel, but had heard of him from her dad. Her dad had told her that he was the young man who had helped at the rallies of the Five Chicano Candidates in the election of 1963, when Mexicans won all the seats on the city council for the first time in history.

Severita was really interested now.

"Please finish the story. This is all so new to me. I went to the games, some of them, but I didn't know anything about this. Really. Tell us," Severita pressed her.

"Well, the MAYO guys told us to forget the walkout because we would flunk . . . that we should not do walkouts in the spring because the teachers just give you zeroes and you fail, and school ends and nothing happens."

"And the tournament?" Severita asked again.

Cuqui explained that she didn't quite know what happened, but before they knew it, the school administration let the students vote on two sets of sweethearts, an Anglo one and a Mexican one. This decision pleased no one but it was a temporary solution to avoid an escalating problem of general Chicano student discontent and dissension among the team's Chicano players.

The school administration's compromise simply fueled the fire already burning among Chicano students. They and all the residents of the city could see the segregation now being made a practice.

Cuqui said, "We asked the MAYO guys if they would come help us at the beginning of the school year in September, because the school administrators would probably do the same thing to us again when it came time to choose cheerleaders, twirlers, drum major, football sweetheart, and homecoming queen. Chicanos always only get one, like I was the only cheerleader. We hardly ever get the sweetheart or the queen. The MAYO guys agreed to come and help out."

Linda blurted out, "We're going to have a walkout when school starts?"

Cuqui ended the conversation without answering the question and instead said, "You know, Armando Treviño is also in Gilroy this summer. His family is working the garlic and apricots around there. You talk to him about what happened, because he was one of the student leaders. He talked more with the MAYO reps. But he's graduated and I don't know if he's coming back to Crystal City."

The rest of the trip was short. California was very pretty— green, cool, and nothing like hot, dry Texas or cold, wet Minnesota. Severita and Linda spent hours viewing the scenery out the car windows. The Moncadas left the Lara girls at the home of their Uncle Nicolás in Gilroy. They had not seen these relatives in a long time, so the next few days were spent talking, eating, and walking downtown in Gilroy. The Lara girls loved Gilroy. They could go to the A&W Root Beer Drive-In, the bowling alley, the Rialto movie theater, and sit anywhere they wanted; there was no Mexican section, like at the Guild Theatre in Crystal City.

Chicano kids in Gilroy spoke really good English and very little Spanish. Many of them couldn't speak it at all. They would say, "I understand it a little bit." Severita and Linda thought this was really odd. Maybe they were just faking because they wanted to pass for Anglos. The Lara girls were confused.

Uncle Nicolás was a supervisor at a cannery, and Severita and Linda bugged him for jobs. It was no fun to stay home while everyone else went to work, and they had no money now. Tío Nico, as they called him, arranged it. Linda did not have as much trouble as Severita with the work, maybe because she had not been ill like her sister. Linda could handle the task of carving out little round balls of melon with little spoons, but Severita could not. She would lose her grip on the spoon and it would fall down the conveyor belt and jam the rollers. After five drops of the spoon and as many jams that backed up the work and stopped production, Tío Nico came and told her they could no longer work there or he would be fired. Severita cried and apologized to Linda for having cost her a job, but Linda was very understanding. She suggested they go work in the fields, like others they knew.

And they did. The girls went out with crews to pick apricots and plums on tall ladders. The fruit would go into a bucket, the buckets were emptied into a box, and they were paid by the box. It took many buckets to fill a box, and each person had to move his own tall, heavy ladder, and carry the bucket up the ladder without falling. Reaching for the fruit was a balancing act sometimes, and some people did fall, including Severita and Linda several times. They just laughed about it, got up, gathered the spilled fruit back into the bucket, and tried again. On other jobs, they had to take the fruit from the boxes—apricots, sometimes grapes, and plums—and lay them out on big screen trays in the sun to dry into prunes and raisins. They would wash and sometimes spray the fruit with sulfur to keep bugs off. The sulfur would hurt their eyes and lungs. It smelled bad. They never knew how prunes and raisins were made until then. They did not even know it was the same fruit, just dried out and shriveled up.

Severita and Linda got sick so many times in Gilroy, not from colds or fevers or pain or being wet and tired, but from eating the fruit they were picking or drying. They went to pick strawberries and ate too many too quickly when they first hit the field one morning; they were back home with diarrhea by midmorning. That crew leader would not take them out again, so they had to find another crew. Even after that, they would eat too many apricots or plums or prunes or raisins and get sick. But they didn't care, they were having fun and making a little money. Every experience was new, and they had Tío Nico to fall back on if things really got bad for them. They had clean sheets, warm water, an indoor toilet and shower, homemade food ready in the evenings and early mornings, time to walk around in Gilroy, and even a dance or two to attend. They had a blast that summer.

They did run into Armando Treviño while walking in town one day and brought up the conversation about the Popeye Tournament and the possible walkout when the school year began. Afterward, over several evening visits, Armando gave them more details about that incident and names of other student leaders to contact when they got back.

He said, "If there is a walkout, you will have to do it, because most of us have graduated. You have to arrange it. We are gone. Work with MAYO."

The Lara girls returned to Crystal City, not with five hundred dollars in their pocket, but with some money and new clothes, plus more gifts for everyone in the family. Soon school started without anything unusual happening. In fact, Severita and Linda both forgot about the walkout business, they were so busy with new class schedules and making more friends. Severita was a junior that year and Linda was a sophomore. Instead of talking about the past injustices surrounding the Popeye Tournament, most juniors were talking about their prom. The junior class was going to be responsible for raising money and sponsoring the prom in April or early May. Linda was busy with the Spanish club, drama, and art. She began to push her favorite sophomores to become prom servers.

The football season and the Friday night rituals began, as in most Texas towns. Everybody stops life and goes to the home game or makes plans, if they can, to travel with their team to a nearby town to cheer their squad. After the home games, the Anglo students had parties in their homes, while the Chicano kids usually hung out at the Dairy Kreme on the corner of East Crockett and North First Avenue, across from the ice plant and the railroad tracks. The railroad tracks were the dividing line between Anglo homes and businesses and the Mexican neighborhood and businesses, although Mexican families were now beginning to live all over the city, on both sides of the tracks and not just in the barrios.

One night at dinner, Chemita mentioned José Angel Gutiérrez was holding meetings with the Mexican men in town about politics. Severita would soon find out what was stirring in the Chicano side of town and in the school board meeting room.

When the homecoming football game approached, Chicano students and football players began asking teachers, coaches, other students and the high school principal about the election. They wanted to know about the candidates and dates for student voting on the homecoming queen. Many a girl, Chicana and Anglo, had private hopes of being a candidate and being chosen. This was not to be for Chicanas.

A group of former Anglo high school graduates had met with several members of the school board and convinced them that a football sweetheart chosen from among those girls whose parents had graduated from the high school was better than a homecoming queen chosen by the students. A majority of the school board members had agreed, so the Ex-Students Crystal City High School Association proceeded to plan for the game activities and selection of the sweetheart.

Severita was furious at this development. It was not fair. Everybody knew that very few Chicano parents had graduated from high school in the 1950s. The Lara parents were not high school graduates. Of the girls they knew, only Diana Serna was eligible. Severita and other students went looking for Armando Treviño and the MAYO people. They found them and were advised to draw up a petition of grievances of how the school treated Chicano students, with demands for reform. They were advised to place the football sweetheart election process at the top of the list. More and more students were recruited by Severita to come talk to the MAYO representatives, who actually were just a young couple, José Angel and Luz Gutiérrez, living in town.

Within a week, after many student meetings and discussions with the MAYO reps, a list of grievances was prepared and signed by about seventy-five Chicano students and taken to the high school principal. He refused it. In essence, he said the football sweetheart selection was not his doing and the list of complaints was not within his power to fix. Everything was decided by the school superintendent and the board of education. Severita asked him to arrange meetings with them. He smirked at her and said that the superintendent probably would not meet with her. She was just a student.

"Ask your parents to call for you," he suggested.

Severita reported that verbal exchange to the students, who now were meeting regularly in homes in groups of ten and twelve. More student signatures were obtained.

Severita went to the superintendent's office and asked for an appointment, but she could not get past the receptionist, an older Anglo woman who wanted to know if her principal knew she was doing this. The receptionist said she would show the list of grievances to the superintendent, but Severita refused to give it to her. She insisted on seeing him in person or getting placed on the agenda of the next school board meeting.

The receptionist said, "Absolutely not. You are a student. No."

Severita stormed out and reviewed in her mind how this exchange had gone. She thought she had done very well. The scenario had unfolded just like her friends from MAYO had predicted. The core student leaders were now meeting regularly with the Gutiérrezes and some other new people, an Anglo couple, Bill and Linda Richey, and Alberto Luera from Laredo. At the time, MAYO was issuing a newspaper, *La Verdad* (The Truth), and was always available for consultation and support. Severita, Mario Treviño, Armando's younger brother and a freshman, Diana Serna, the younger sister of another graduate, Libby, were the core leadership. They started hanging around the Gutiérrez household almost daily. MAYO members predicted what the school authorities would do and say almost to the word. They coached Severita. MAYO members had a lot of experience—they'd been organizing school protests and walkouts in Texas since 1967.

When the petition process failed, the students were encouraged to print a leaflet, calling for a meeting at the Salón Campestre to discuss the issues and develop a plan of action. The homecoming game was rapidly approaching. The leaflet was prepared but nobody wanted to distribute it at school; they were all afraid of being suspended. Severita said she would do it.

The next day, the assistant high school principal, Paulino Mata, the first Mexican American to hold such a position, spied her coming into the school building with the petitions. He watched her pass out the first few and moved in quickly, trying to grab them out of her hand, but he was not fast enough. Severita had seen him coming. He was a large guy, as big as the principal at about 6 feet 3 inches and 240 pounds. She just turned as he grabbed, and he ended up hitting her on the back with his hand. He apologized and was on the defensive from then on. Severita started demanding he stop attacking her and let her exercise her right to pass out the leaflets.

He turned very red in the face and tightened his mouth. All he said was, "Give me one."

With the leaflets in hand, he marched off to report her to the principal. Severita knew what was next. Sure enough, Principal John B. Lair came almost running out of his office.

"Not on school grounds, young lady. Not on my campus. Stop. Stop. You give me those leaflets," he yelled.

He also tried to grab out of her hands. But Severita had been coached properly. She just turned her back and clutched the leaflets to her chest, wrapped by both arms.

Students coming into the school saw the altercation. They wanted the petitions, and Severita continued to give them to some students and asked them to pass them out in their classes. By the time Lair was able to stop her, Severita had passed out about half of the pile. Principal Lair, with help from Mata, literally grabbed Severita by her elbows and lifted her into the air. As they carried her into the office, Severita managed to drop some more leaflets in the hallway. Students raced for them like candy falling out of a piñata. Lair was so angry, his glasses fogged up. He grabbed the petitions and tore them out of Severita's clutches.

"Young lady, you are suspended. No student comes into this building to disrupt the school program. You are not going to spread propaganda in my building. Severita, you are a rabble-rouser!"

Severita started for the door. "Come back here. Right now! Come back here," is what she last heard, but Severita kept on walking into the hallway and out the front door. To students she met on the way out she said, "I'm suspended. Lair ran me off."

When Severita reached her dad's gas station at mid-morning, her dad quizzed her. Satisfied with her story, Chemita, said, "Do it, *m'ijita*, I'm with you. If you know it's right, do it." Severita then called the MAYO members and did not have to explain much. They immediately got on the telephone and obtained legal assistance from the Mexican American Legal Defense and Educational Fund (MALDEF). A lawyer would come to Crystal City in a day or two. The MAYO reps encouraged Severita to print more leaflets and pass them out in the morning from the sidewalk in front of the school. One of the MAYO members suggested she wear a black armband on her right arm. The armband would symbolize mourning for the death of the First Amendment to the U.S. Constitution at Crystal City High School. She got the idea behind that symbolic gesture right away. She was learning that protest can be harmful to a person, but it was fun and the right thing to do. She and many Chicano students watched adults behave badly while insisting that what they taught about government and democracy was true—just not at Crystal City High School while they were in charge.

Early the next morning, MALDEF's attorney, Gerald "Jerry" López came into town in his nicely pressed dark blue suit and bright red tie. It took him less than one day to argue with the superintendent and phone other lawyers inside that office. López emerged smiling.

He told Severita that she had been reinstated and could pass out her leaflets and any other printed matter from the sidewalk and in the school hallways before, after, and during lunch.

"And don't get caught if you do it between classes. I may not be able to come back until next week."

Severita did just that, with her black armband still on her arm. Students were in awe of her. She had fought the system and won! They all began to rally behind her leadership.

The student meeting at the Salón Campestre came off like a charm. Severita spoke first and repeated the entire list of grievances, and reviewed the leaflet incident in great detail. She announced that Chicano students were tired of second-class treatment and discrimination. They wanted action! She encouraged those in attendance to support the drawing up of student demands, not just a list of grievances, but demands. She asked for the crowd to vote on attending the next school board meeting to demand that the homecoming queen not be selected by ex-students. The crowd roared. It was made up mostly of students, but a few parents were present, as well as the MAYO representative. Armando Treviño also spoke about the incident of the Popeye Tournament sweetheart from the previous spring. He encouraged the crowd to keep up the fight and stop the homecoming queen election process.

Over the next three weeks, the school board met in a regular session and one emergency session. The result was the same at each meeting. The school board first refused to meet with Chicano students and discuss their demands. The board president, Ed Mayer, insisted these matters be taken care of by the respective administrators in charge: the principals, superintendent, head coach, teachers, and the like. The students were run out of the meeting and told to bring their parents. The school board was not going to discuss matters with students, only with parents. This was an old trick: to deal with parents who were very vulnerable to the Anglo business owners, farmers, and ranchers. Ed Mayer himself was an executive at the Del Monte plant. Any parent showing up at the school board meeting might lose his job at the plant.

Despite these dangers, brave parents did come, mostly mothers, to the next school board meeting, but they too were dismissed by the board without discussing their demands. Finally, the fathers and mothers and students all came together to the board meeting. Nothing different happened at this meeting. In fact, at this meeting, the school board instructed the staff to remove all chairs from the meeting room. The people had to stand. It was a big mistake. Instead of the Chicanos being uncomfortable in standing, the school board members became uncomfortable with so many people standing around them, upon them, next to them, and all over them. The president adjourned the meeting because everyone was talking at the same time and he could not maintain order. The board did not really want to discuss the demands. As soon as the school board members left the room and hid in the superintendent's office, Chicano parents and their kids left the building.

Outside, Severita seized the opportunity. She was handed a handheld megaphone and began speaking to the parents. "See what we are dealing with? You came to be heard and they ignored you. We are ignored and treated just like that every day. This should not be a school just for Anglos. It should be for us also. If we can't get a fair break, then no one should. What should we do?"

Severita had not finished her last question when other Chicano students with clenched fists in the air started chanting, "Walk out! Walk out! Walk out!"

The parents began to nod in agreement and soon were mouthing the new words in their vocabulary: "Walk out! Walk out!"

Change was in the air. Crystal City would never be the same. Severita was the leader in charge.

The next morning, on December 9, 1969, history was made. It was the first morning of the walkout. For the next twenty-nine days, including the Christmas holidays and New Year, until January 7, 1970, Chicano students of Crystal City began boycotting classes. The first few days, just a few hundred walked out. Some of the students were told specifically not to walk out, so they could bring home the class assignments, class notes, and homework to those in the walkout. Every morning before classes began, Chicano students boycotting would march up the steps of the high school, and two of them would go inside and ask for the nation's flag to raise it. Those protesting would recite the Pledge of Allegiance. When the principal tried to prevent that from happening, the television cameras and other news reporters were present, so he could not refuse. He was losing this fight from the first day. Chicano students knew what they were doing. Parents were recruited to bring hot drinks and snacks to those protesting with signs on the sidewalk in front of the school. Every day another hundred or so students more would walk out. Marches from the high school to the downtown area were held right after the morning patriotic ceremony. The number of protestors reached 1,700 and spread to every school and grade level in the entire district.

During the Christmas break, Chicano teachers and administrators, even two superintendents, came to teach classes at a barrio school set up by MAYO reps. Classses were held for the boycotting students in empty halls, businesses, bars, churches, and outdoors in the Juan García Park and at La Placita. At these classes, Chicano students learned about their history, culture, language, heritage, and prior civil rights struggles. They learned of César Chávez and Reies López Tijerina. They learned about the Five Chicano Candidates and their valiant effort in 1963. During spare time, when the students were not marching, protesting, studying, singing, and reciting the pledge, MAYO members asked them to go house to house in the barrios to explain the purpose of the walkout to every

Chicano family. They also registered voters. When all Chicanos in Crystal City were registered to vote, the students moved on to La Pryor and Batesville in the county, then other cities nearby. Anglos in these other cities got angry with the Anglos in Crystal City because they did not want similar events in their towns. Crystal City's Anglos were getting very bad press in the newspapers from San Antonio. They seemed unreasonable while Chicano students only to wanted an education. Anglos were very upset they had to cancel their plans to crown their Anglo homecoming sweetheart on the football field. She was crowned in an onion shed. Downtown businesses were losing money because of the constant marches and demonstrations.

To escalate matters, Severita and Linda were both arrested by the local sheriff for picketing a grocery store, Speer's Minimax. Severita was arrested for picketing and Linda for grabbing the sheriff's arm when he started to manhandle her sister.

"Let her go. Let her go. She didn't do anything," Linda shouted as she grabbed him by the arm.

The grocery store owner, J.L. Speer, had fired a Chicano student for participating in the walkout. The response of Chicano students was like that of the Three Musketeers: "All for one, one for all." If anyone harmed any protesting student, all students would come to their rescue. When Cleofas Támez, another student protestor, was arrested by the sheriff, the same response occurred. Students would march to the courthouse en masse. MALDEF lawyers and other supportive Chicano attorneys, such as Mike González from Del Rio, would immediately respond when summoned. In both cases, Severita, Linda, and Cleofas were released within hours by the sheriff because of the immense pressure from the shouting, demonstrating students outside the building and the threatened legal action by Chicano attorneys. The sheriff had arrested the juveniles on ridiculous charges—and without notifying their parents.

The student core leaders would huddle nightly at the Gutiérrez house to review the happenings of the day and make new plans for the next days. Parents were kept informed at Ciudadanos Unidos

(United Citizens) meetings and the weekly public rallies held by the students. Severita, Diana, Mario, and sometimes other nonstudents would speak to the crowds. Severita was always excellent. She had a way with words. Her body frame was small, but not her voice. It carried, and her eyes communicated. She had passion and tremendous courage. Severita, Diana, and Mario were everywhere coordinating, leading, directing, speaking, organizing, analyzing, discussing, planning, and, most importantly, following through with the plans.

When the local media seemed to lose interest in covering this prolonged protest, the student leaders met to discuss how to reach a statewide audience. Pressure had to continue on the school board because it was still adamant about not discussing—much less negotiating—the demands with students. The local MAYO members contacted the state MAYO headquarters in San Antonio, and one of the leaders, Juan Patlán, immediately arranged a trip to Washington, D.C., for the three Chicano student leaders.

Severita, Diana, and Mario flew to the nation's capital. Having given so many speeches and answered so many questions from reporters, the trio had become professionals in speaking to the press. Severita, the junior class member, was the main speaker over the two freshmen, Mario and Diana. They were met at Dulles International Airport by Senator Ralph W. Yarborough's staff. The three of them were given a tour of the city and the Capitol. They met with Senator Edward Kennedy. The only interested and gracious Republican member of Congress to meet with them was George H.W. Bush, the representative from Houston, Texas. He made it possible for the trio to meet with the assistant secretary of Health, Education, and Welfare and representatives of the Department of Justice. Congressman Bush was instrumental in involving the Community Relations Service, a conflict mediation agency of the Department of Justice. The elected officials helped the Chicano students get appointments with government officials of the highest rank in the Richard Nixon administration. The government officials in turn all promised to investigate the school boycott in Crystal City.

It was a major victory for all students that Severita, Mario, and Diana were bringing home. If the Anglo school board and administration were to be investigated by federal officials, they would discover the wrongs. When the three Chicano students came home, they received a hero's welcome, beginning at the San Antonio airport. A caravan of cars led them back to Crystal City triumphantly. They had taken and delivered the Chicano message to the nation. Stories about them had come out in the major national newspapers. The whole world knew what was happening in Crystal City, Texas. The town was on the map. At the public rally that night, the mood was one of extreme joy and empowerment. Severita, Diana, and Mario took their time narrating each interview, each visit, each conversation, they had had with the people in Washington, D.C. The crowd interrupted them with applause constantly. Every person listening felt proud of these brave Chicanos. Parents in attendance were beaming with pride because their children were a part of this.

The promises made by Washington politicians and officials were promises kept. Federal investigators from the Department of Justice's Community Relations Service; the Civil Rights Commission; Health, Education, and Welfare; and even the state Texas Education Agency came to town to investigate. The school board and superintendent did not know when they would have time to conduct business, they were so busy answering embarrassing questions. The newspapers and television stations that covered Crystal City seemed to have a new story a day. They reported their comings and they reported on their goings, and they reported on everything that happened. Crystal City's walkout was on the front page of every Texas newspaper.

Soon after the beginning of class in the new year of 1970, the school board realized that the boycott was going to continue. Chicano students were not returning to classes unless their demands were met. Both the federal authorities and the Texas Education Agency could not understand why the school board refused to meet to discuss the demands. The striking students seemed ready to talk since before the protest, in fact, that was what caused the walkout in the first place: the school board's refusal to discuss, negotiate, and agree on terms.

Local businesses could not understand why the school board did not resolve the matter. It was bad for business. Anglo leaders from neighboring communities were growing more concerned that Chicanos in their communities might emulate Chicanos in Crystal City. And the voter registration drives continued.

The school board caved in to the pressure from Washington, Austin, local officials, businesses, and the press. It finally agreed to negotiate the demands. Chicano students realized that who their negotiators were would determine how much they won. Severita called a meeting of students and parents. They chose their negotiators carefully. The students told those selected which were the priority demands and which were those they could live without for the time being. Severita rattled them off: bilingual education, Chicano teachers, Chicano books, amnesty for the protestors, Chicano food in the cafeteria, Chicano workers in the school district, Chicano school counselors, student-controlled elections for everything, and on and on. . . .

Over the course of tense day and late-night sessions, the negotiating team and the school board hammered out an agreement that both sides could live with. The school board felt it had won. The students would again be under their control and they had not promised to meet the demands by certain dates, just that they would try. Chicano kids and parents felt they had won. They had made the school board accept their terms. They had proved that Chicanos in Crystal City could make the system bend to their will. The settlement made the local, state, and national news.

Severita, Mario, and Diana were considered heroes in town. When they returned to classes, teachers treated them with kid gloves.

Severita and the other student leaders kept in contact with MAYO. They all continued to work on La Verdad newspaper and formed their own youth organization, the Youth Association (YA). They had learned so much so quickly. They wanted to learn more. They were curious about the plans for organizing a political party to take control of the school board, city council, and all of Zavala County.

Severita at age 4, Crystal City, TX.

Severita with her brother and sister in Crystal City, TX.

From left to right: Mario Treviño, Severita, Diana Serna, and U.S. Senator Ralph Yarbrough in Washington, D.C. when students went to discuss Crystal City schools.

From left to right: Ramón de la Fuente, Jaime María Lara, Severita, Esequiel, Irene Lara, and Elvira de la Fuente on Severita and Esequiel's wedding day.

Severita Lara headquarters, Crystal City, TX, 1986.

Severita Lara speaking to the community.

Chapter 5
Baby Kiki and the Thunderbird

Severita was the talk of the town, the real heroine of the student walkout. Everyone praised and complimented her on her excellent leadership skills. The students and parents did not stop with the negotiated victory with the school board. The MAYO advisors had pointed out that the demands now conceded were nothing but words on a piece of paper. The Chicano community understood that in order to make the victory last, it had to continue to remain united and to organize voters to take control of the school board with candidates of their choosing. Perhaps the Chicano community could even elect a new city council and county government.

On January 10, 1970, at a giant rally in the Salón Campestre, various speakers, including Severita and such older women as Virginia Múzquiz, recommended the forming of a new political party, La Raza Unida (The United People). In the final days of the walkout negotiations, the newly formed community organization, Ciudadanos Unidos (United Citizens), had already discussed the next step in assuring that Chicano community control would be realized. Plans were made to form the political party. Severita and the other student leaders were too young to run and hold public office, so Ciudadanos Unidos voted to find candidates for the school board and other governmental entities, but first they wanted broader community support. Ciudadanos Unidos allowed full membership to anyone over the age of 16. Students had a vote on all decisions at those meetings and felt they were equal partners with their parents and other community elders. Chicanos were all very optimistic that they would win the election if they stayed together and received the vote for their candidates.

Ciudadanos Unidos began that process during large meetings held on Sundays at noon, often lasting well into midafternoon. Candidates were selected. All the people who had registered to vote needed to come to the polls in the April elections for the school board and the city council. Severita and the hundreds of other students involved in the walkout, together with their parents, became the campaign organization for their Chicano candidates. Every Sunday after the Ciudadanos Unidos meeting, the membership went out to walk the streets, knocking on doors, asking for support for their candidates.

The political rallies and meetings were lots of fun for the students. Severita and others would work on selling advertisements and writing stories for *La Verdad* newspaper, they walked the streets on weekends, they obtained signatures for the petition to get the Raza Unida Party on the local ballot, and they celebrated often after the rallies, block parties, and cookouts held by supporters in their back yards to raise money for the various candidates.

Some of the most well-known Chicano musicians, such as Little Joe y La Familia, Augustín Ramírez, The Tortilla Factory, and Laura Canales, came to play benefits for La Raza Unida Party and Ciudadanos Unidos. Dancing was a favorite pastime for Severita and her boyfriend, Esequiel de la Fuente.

Partying and dancing got Severita and Esequiel in trouble on a Friday night. They had permission to go to the Augustín Ramírez dance being held at the Pan American Ballroom, sponsored by Mike Pérez, one of the school board candidates of Ciudadanos Unidos. Severita's mother, still a very strict disciplinarian, would punish her if she came in after her curfew. Her mother did not care how important Severita had been to the success of the community in the walkout and now the campaigns for public office. She would still beat her if she did not obey the house rules. During the walkout and the meetings, her mother would let her stay out a bit later, but not often. Now that the walkout was over, politics was not Severita's business, her mother would tell her. The Augustín Ramírez dance was not an excuse to stay out late.

Severita had grown tired of the rigid rules and physical attacks by her mother. She had proven she was responsible for months during the walkout and in the campaign work underway. She was a good girl and never did anything wrong. Her mother had to stop trying to control her and her sister Linda.

Severita and Esequiel stopped to eat after the dance and started home after 1:30 in the morning. When they realized what time it was, Severita knew she was going to get a beating. She told Esequiel she did not want to go home. They did not know where to go and decided to sleep in Esequiel's pickup in the Juan García Park. They would face her mother in the morning. Severita knew her dad would understand; it was her mother that was going to be the problem.

Severita's parents were really worried when she did not come home. They called Esequiel's parents, only to find out he had not come home either. Both sets of the parents knew they had run away together. Severita's Aunt Felicita, who happened to be visiting from California, volunteered to go in search of the couple and found them at the park about 3 a.m. sound asleep in the truck. She knocked on the window until they opened it. Felicita tried to convince Severita to come home, but she refused. She told her aunt about the beatings and how she was not going to accept that anymore. She would rather live somewhere else. She and Esequiel never did anything wrong, she told her aunt. Felicita convinced the couple to at least go to Esequiel's home, because they too were worried about him, and that tomorrow she would help Severita with her mother and father. So, taking her aunt's advice, the couple went to Esequiel's parents' home. Things were a little better there. His parents were very religious and disciplinarians, too, but never beat the children except for an occasional smack on the hand or butt to make a point.

The next morning, Esequiel and Severita went to face her

mother at her house. Her mother was livid and, thank goodness, her dad and aunt were there, because she tried to hit Severita several times. She had to be restrained.

"You have brought shame to our entire family," she shouted while trying to grab Severita from behind Esequiel.

Above her mother's yelling, Severita would shout back, "We didn't do anything. Nothing happened."

Chemita, the voice of reason asked, "Do you want to get married? If you are going to have a baby, that's no reason to get married. We can always feed another mouth here."

"No, Dad, I haven't done anything, and I don't want to get married," Severita told him.

Still trying to grab Severita from behind Esequiel, her mother was shouting, "Just let me catch you, I'm going to give it to you good!"

Esequiel knew the situation was getting worse and worse. Nothing was going to work out, and he was not going to leave Severita there alone. He said, "We're going to get married. I love her, and you are not going to hit her."

Severita and Esequiel backed out of the house and into his truck and sped off. Severita cried all the way to his house.

Esequiel's mom and dad insisted they marry within days, and arranged for a private wedding at Severita's house after assuring her parents that the couple could stay with them. Chemita wanted to know how his daughter was going to be taken care of by Esequiel, since he was attending the community college in Uvalde. Esequiel promised he would find a job, finish school, and take good care of her.

The couple was married by Justice of the Peace Julián Salas at the Lara home with a few family members and the godparents they had chosen—José Angel and his wife, Luz, the MAYO organizers. Within a week, the couple also had a church wedding.

Severita continued attending classes at the high school—she was still a junior—and Esequiel finished his semester at the junior college in Uvalde. The couple dropped out of attending the

Ciudadanos Unidos meetings and would make an occasional rally, but life was different now for both of them. Severita did not have time to take care of her husband because she had to get herself to school early. Esequiel left for his school even earlier and worked late helping his father with his gasoline station and engine repairs. Like Severita's father, Ramón de la Fuente had a gas station and they stayed open late. That is why Esequiel never had much time for Severita. But they were together and in love. Severita missed the excitement of the campaign and the meetings, and her friends as well. She was now a married woman.

Even when the Ciudadanos Unidos slate of candidates won both the school board and city council elections, Severita and Esequiel did not attend the victory celebrations, because they felt different and out of place. Her godparents, Luz and José Angel, scolded her, telling her, "You have ruined your life! You had such a bright future! You did not have to marry and you do not have to have a baby."

But no one had even told Severita about sex, and she was pregnant before school was out. She had worked as a candy striper at the local medical clinic and knew about health care, and preventive medicine, but not about birth control.

Meanwhile, Esequiel received a draft notice for the war in Vietnam. They talked about their future when they could and in whispers, because the time they had together was late at night and there were too many people in the de la Fuente household. Severita wanted a place of her own to begin a life with Esequiel and the baby.

Severita talked with her mother-in-law about helping her move into a place of her own. She understood and agreed. The problem was Severita had not discussed it with Esequiel. Being the assertive person that she still was, she borrowed money from Elvira and Ramón, and moved to a home about to be vacated by the Cárdenas family, who was ready to go north in search of work. Ramón helped Severita move out and into the new home. When Esequiel returned from classes at the community college that evening, he found out and was very angry. He refused to move in with her. For several days, he stayed away and continued to live with his parents until he realized he had to start a life on his own.

Severita's last days in school were horrible: she suffered morning sickness because of the pregnancy. She would not see Esequiel until late at night. Every day it was same routine, and on weekends Esequiel would work at the gas station during the day and spend time with his friends in the evening. Severita suggested they move to San Antonio so he could finish at the university and she could go to school, too. She had begun to realize she had made a very big mistake. She had always wanted to become a medical doctor when she grew up, but that prospect seemed very distant now.

After Esequiel finished his first two years of college at Uvalde, he got a job at Del Monte, and Severita resumed her work with *La Verdad* newspaper. She also worked with a new organization that had formed to spur economic development among Chicanos in Crystal City: the Texas Institute for Educational Development (TIED). During that summer, Severita filled out the paperwork to get Esequiel a military deferment and applications for both of them to attend St. Mary's University in San Antonio. At the end of summer, with the few dollars they had saved, the couple decided to move to San Antonio. Severita hadn't finish high school. Esequiel was accepted into St. Mary's University and got his deferment because of Severita's paperwork.

Luz Gutiérrez, the godmother for her marriage ceremony, gave Severita an opportunity to become one of her trainers in an early childhood program. Luz worked for the Colorado Migrant Council (CMC), which was sending people for training to Our Lady of the Lake College in San Antonio so that they could return and help run Head Start centers for migrant children in South Texas. Things were looking up for the couple. Esequiel was going to finish college and Severita was going to start her career.

The couple bought an old Ford Galaxy for $75, packed the

few things they owned, and drove to San Antonio early one August morning just before classes were to start. They had only $150 dollars in savings and a few more bucks to spare. Esequiel drove to St. Mary's University and found it near the West Side barrio. Fortunately, Our Lady of the Lake College was also nearby. They inquired about housing in a few places that had "For Rent" signs, but they were too expensive. The couple did not have enough for rent or the deposits to turn on the electricity, water, gas, and sewer. Their first night in San Antonio was spent in the car.

Every night for the next two weeks was spent in the car. Sometimes they slept in front of Good Samaritan Community Center, where Severita's program was located, sometimes they slept in parking lots, and other occasions when the police came by, they slept at all-night gas stations. Severita and Esequiel would rise with the sun and shower in the community center before anyone else got up. Esequiel would drop her off at Our Lady of the Lake, then go to St. Mary's for his classes. They ate what they could when they could, trying to keep as much of the $150 as possible, but it was dwindling fast to pay for food and gas. Esequiel would pick her up in the late afternoon, and they would again go in search of affordable housing. Nothing was affordable.

One of Severita's professors, Dr. Patrick Bone, made it a point to visit his students at home. She put him off every week until he insisted she had to invite him over because she was the only one remaining on his list.

She broke down and told him, "I cannot take you to my home because I do not have one. I sleep in a car with my husband."

He was in shock. He demanded to see for himself. Esequiel was very embarrassed when she told him about the professor's insistence and imminent visit. It turned out to be a blessing.

Dr. Bone met Esequiel and Severita at their car and he insisted they go immediately to the San Antonio Housing Authority with him in his car and get public housing. He had contacts. Dr.

Bone took them inside the offices, and they filled out applications. When the professor found out Severita was pregnant, he pleaded with the director to let them have anything available. Dr. Bone was very persistent.

Thanks to Dr. Bone, Severita and Esequiel were able to get an unfurnished apartment for $7 a month. They were ecstatic about their good luck. Dr. Bone even brought them an iron antique bed from one of his relatives. Slowly, they got pieces of furniture from others to make the place somewhat comfortable. Severita went to Goodwill Industries and bought secondhand dishes, linen, and appliances. They finally were living like a normal couple in their own apartment.

Dr. Bone would visit them regularly, always with a bag of groceries of vegetables and fruit, even meat sometimes, for Severita. Once he inquired about her prenatal care and Severita looked at him blankly. Severita never dreamed she would become pregnant so soon and had not made any plans for having the baby.

The professor took her to fill out applications not only for food stamps but also the Women, Infants, and Children Program (WIC). He insisted she get a medical checkup. She followed his advice and kept her appointments with these agencies and the doctor, but made up her mind to have her baby in Crystal City—she would save money by paying for it to be born there. Esequiel agreed with her and took two jobs on top of his college work to save money. He worked at a convenience store and at the university library.

As the semester was ending, the couple had saved up and already paid $450 for the baby's birth in Crystal City. Two days before the end of the semester, Severita began to feel cramps and knew the impending birth was days away. Her mother, during that ugly episode when she and Esequiel had come home the morning after the dance, had yelled at her, "You're going to die of pain when you give birth, you ingrate. You'll scream and suffer and cry for being such a spoiled brat."

Esequiel had already finished his semester exams by the time

Severita took her last one on a Saturday. That night she could not sleep. She hurt everywhere. She tried to sleep on this side and that side, but the pain from cramps was too great. She kept going to the bathroom every few minutes and did not even notice her water had broken. She seemed wet between her legs all night long. Finally, she woke Esequiel and told him they had better drive to Crystal City because she was having the baby.

The old Galaxy had died a month earlier, and on a trip home, Esequiel had borrowed another car. Severita had been concerned about the clunker when he drove up with it. She laughed even more when she saw three spare tires in the trunk, but then began to worry. The tires were very worn out. Nevertheless, the car ran, not more than 40 miles per hour, but it got them here and there. The trip that Saturday night to Crystal City was going to be another matter. The tires had better hold out and the car had better go faster than 40 miles an hour, because she was having the baby. The San Antonio doctor had advised against the trip just days before when he had examined Severita, but he had the foresight to tell Esequiel what to do in case of an emergency. He even gave Esequiel scissors, an umbilical clamp, and gauze for the eventuality of a surprise birthing.

The couple took off just after midnight. Esequiel chose to go down I-35 to Cotulla and then turn across to Crystal City instead of taking the shortcut. If they needed emergency care, Severita could get it in the towns off the freeway. The only stretch without towns was about 45 miles long. They risked it.

They made it at 40 miles an hour to Cotulla with Severita screaming all the way because of the painful cramps. After about two hours, when they hit the back road from Cotulla to Big Wells, they had their first flat tire. Esequiel worked as fast as he could to change the tire, with Severita holding the flashlight so he could see what he was doing. He would yell at her to hold it steady and she would scream back between cramps and shaking that she was doing the best she could. After fixing the tire, Severita laid down on the back seat, and Esequiel hurriedly drove on.

Past Big Wells near Brundage, just a junction in the back road, they had another flat. Again, Esequiel worked desperately, changing the tire in the dark and demanding that Severita hold the light steady. She kept screaming back, "I can't. I'm not going to make it. Hurry!"

Somehow the second tire was put in place in record time and off they went again. Esequiel had his foot pressed on the gas pedal, but the car would not go faster than 40 miles per hour. It was just too old.

Just past the railroad switch, in an unincorporated area on the edge of Crystal City about 5 miles from downtown, another tire blew. There were no more spare tires. By now there was some dawn light, but Severita could not get out of the back seat. She was screaming in pain "Please, God, not yet. Help my child be born well. Hurry, Esequiel."

Esequiel was scared. He did not want to deliver his own baby at the edge of town. He cursed himself for not having been more concerned and informed about having a baby. It was too late. The baby was about to be born.

With flat tire and all, Esequiel drove straight to the Winter Garden Hospital and Clinic. He ran into the facility and asked them to call Dr. Donald Smith because his wife was having a baby in the car. The staff rushed out and helped Severita into a gurney and rolled her into the birthing area. The staff took over and pushed Esequiel aside. He protested to no avail. They told him that he had done good in bringing her to the hospital, but now he needed to go away. He had waited too long, they said— the baby's head was visible! They had to hurry and prepare her for the delivery.

Severita was screaming louder now. Esequiel could hear her; he was right outside the delivery room. And the doctor had arrived. He kept asking Severita to push and to cry if she needed to. Esequiel was shocked to hear his wife say, "No! I will not cry. I will not have tears. No one will see me cry." She also yelled for him not to contact the family.

Esequiel was torn as to what to do. On the one hand, he wanted to call the relatives and tell them Severita was having a baby. On the other he did not want to go against her wishes and have them come to see her in labor. He knew that Severita was the strongest-willed woman he had ever met. Severita did not want her own mother there to see her cry. He opted for not calling anyone and just waited.

Within minutes, Dr. Smith came out and dropped his hygienic facial mask. He was smiling. He said, "Dad, you have a beautiful boy. In a bit, you'll see your wife. She did very well. I am surprised at how strong she is. The baby is fine. Go get some sleep after you see her because she will sleep for a long time."

Esequiel did get to see Severita, but only for a moment. She raised her hand and lightly waved. She was overcome with exhaustion. He kissed her forehead as they wheeled her out. He went home but did not sleep. He told his parents of the ordeal with the flats in driving in and thanked his father for having put all three spares in the trunk. Then, Esequiel started calling everyone he knew, including Severita's parents, to tell them he had a son and that Severita was in the local hospital doing just fine.

By late morning, Severita was awake and had met her son. Family and friends began taking turns meeting the newborn and congratulating Severita. The baby boy was 19 inches long and weighed 6 pounds. She named him Esequiel Junior, even though Esequiel had asked Severita not to.

Esequiel went back to San Antonio to work his store job over the semester break and Christmas holidays. Chemita came to take Severita home, but Severita requested he take her to Elvira's home, not his. She could see how that hurt him very much, but Severita still had issues with her mother. Besides, her mom and dad had just had a another baby, Rolando, after twelve years since the birth of her youngest sister, Yolanda. Rolando, her baby brother, was only a year and seven months older than her own son.

Within days, Severita asked her godmother, Luz, to allow her to start her job at the local day care center for migrant children.

Severita needed the money. Severita would rise very early, breast-feed her baby and go to work. And every two hours, she would walk home to breast-feed Esequiel Jr. Occasionally, she would go by her family home and offer to take Rolando, her baby brother, out for a while to give her mother a much needed break. Her mother still did not like to go out of the house. She was also embarrassed that she had had a baby as an older woman. People in town would see Severita and ask her if that was the baby they heard she had.

"No, this is my brother. My baby was just born. He is at home with Elvira."

Some people did not believe her, choosing instead to think she had dropped out of school and out of sight because she had gotten pregnant right after the walkout.

At the end of May, Severita rejoined her husband in San Antonio. Her neighbor at the Viramendi Courts, Señora Josefa Silvestre, offered to care for Kiki, as she had nicknamed Esequiel Jr. Severita and Esequiel had finally moved from the apartment after a year and a half. Señora Silvestre and Severita became good friends. She taught Severita how to care for a child. She taught her to make home remedies when the baby cried from colic or diarrhea. She showed her how to bathe him and put him to sleep. She taught her a lot of things a young woman only learns from an older mentor, even how to make flour tortillas. Señora Silvestre was a seamstress and made many nice clothes and outfits for Severita and the baby. Severita had only watched these things done at her house. She was beginning to understand how privileged she had been in her childhood.

Severita was determined to continue her education and enrolled at St. Mary's University. She and her husband would go to school together; Esequiel was seeking a degree in political science and Severita still wanted to be a medical doctor. Esequiel finished his course work ahead of her in 1974. She had at least a year to go, but he would not wait on her. He wanted them to move back to Crystal City because he had a job offer to direct the new mental health program. Severita refused to interrupt her education again. She knew that if she did not finish her degree program then, she never would. So Esequiel left her and the baby in San Antonio.

St. Mary's University discovered that Severita had not finished high school, yet she was in their school and doing really well. She had excellent grades. The man in charge of admissions called her in and insisted she take her high school equivalency tests so that he would not be accused of helping her out by making exceptions. Severita took the exams and passed without a problem, but she also decided to transfer to Incarnate Word College and get her degree in biology.

With Esequiel gone, Severita had to take a job with the Mexican American Unity Council under the direction of Juan Patlán, the MAYO member who had helped her with the trip to Washington, D.C., during the walkout. Severita graduated in 1976 and returned to Crystal City for a job with the local manpower programs. She tried to form a family with Esequiel again, but he had been alone too long. He preferred to spend time with his friends. Severita got a divorce from him in 1976 because he did not want to help her support their son. Severita had money saved up and bought the first new car in her life, a Thunderbird.

She gave up on her dream of becoming a doctor until her godmother, Luz Gutiérrez, called her and sent her an application for a new program the Raza Unida Party had started with the government of Mexico. The Mexican government was going to provide scholarships for Chicanos to become doctors and care for Mexicans as well as Chicanos in the United States.

Severita had to make another of those crossroad decisions in her life. Stay in Crystal City to make enough money to raise her son or pursue her dream, even if Kiki had to face poverty again. Scholarships are wonderful, but they pay only for books or tuition (or sometimes both), but what of living expenses, child care, and health insurance?

The passion in her heart for becoming a medical doctor was too great. She had made many mistakes early in life. She had to gamble and take risks once again. She would not be able to live with herself if she did not try. She realized that opportunity only knocks on your door once. You take it or leave it. She took it.

Within days, Severita was making arrangements to go to Mexico to study medicine. She never once thought of leaving Kiki behind. He was going with her. They would find a way to make it.

Chapter 6
Going Back to Mexico

Within days Severita was on an airplane headed for Mexico City's El Diplomático Hotel for the group orientation of the Becas Para Aztlán Program, the scholarship program that would prepare her for medicine. The taxi ride from Mexico City's international airport was the craziest escapade she had ever experienced. First of all, the taxi was a tiny Volkswagen Beetle without a passenger's seat. It wasn't missing, it was just not there, so that passengers could easily get in and out of the back seat. Secondly, the driver weaved in and out of traffic at zooming speeds. She held on for dear life. She felt like a bouncing ball in a pinball machine: tilt, tilt, tilt. And the city was humongous. The Beetle lurched on green lights and came to screeching halts on red lights. Policemen with whistles in their mouths or gloved hands were everywhere, and it seemed as if no one noticed them, much less paid attention to them. They blew and blew their whistles at everyone, and no one seemed to pay attention. She saw blocks and blocks of streets, stores, shops, wall-to-wall people, cars, bicycles, mopeds, carts, peddlers on every street corner hawking gum, Kleenex, fruit, flowers, toys, and others selling tacos, *licuados, tortas,* and *fruta con chile* as the driver manuevered her deeper and deeper into the city. Severita marveled at the giant statues everywhere of Lincoln, Benito Juárez, Napoleon, Julius Caesar, George Washington, and Montezuma. Severita was astonished with amazement at the architecture, monuments, and thousands of people. This was the real Mexico, she thought, not the border culture she knew in Piedras Negras-Eagle Pass. Ever-present reminders of the Mexican Revolution of 1910 were everywhere on street names, like the wide avenue they were on, Insurgentes. At another screeching halt, the driver announced calmly, "El Diplomático," as he nodded to his right and jumped out to help Severita from the backseat, still clutching her overnight bag and purse. She paid him in dollars because she had not made time to exchange currency at the airport.

Inside the hotel lobby Severita got lost among the hundreds of young people milling around. As she headed for the registration desk, the sound of Spanglish greeted her, and she realized that these were potential students like her. These were *becarios*, as the Chicano scholarship recipients were called by Mexicans. They had come from all over the United States.

Over the course of three days and the filling out of thirty different forms, the *becarios* received instructions on how to collect their scholarship money, move into their rental homes, and attend the university locations across the country. They also had an intensive workshop on how Mexico worked, from government to society. Not all the Chicano students were going to the same university; they were assigned all over Mexico. Severita got Mexico City's Universidad Metropolitana Autónoma with an address for her rental home in Xochimilco Country Club in an area of the city she could not pronounce. Severita was fascinated with these indigenous names. She would roll the words around in her mouth to practice their pronunciation.

Severita met her future housemates, the Orozco sisters, Irma and Cynthia, from Cuero, Texas; Cristina López from San Fernando, California; Marta Franco from El Paso, Texas; and Bárbara Reyes from San Antonio. They made sure they wrote down their new address and projected a date to rendezvous at that location within a few days.

Severita was so excited on the flight back to Texas. She was going to go to medical school and come back to Crystal City and be known as Dr. Lara. She would care for her father, who had had a stroke in 1975 while she was finishing college.

Kiki was withdrawn from day care in Crystal City, their few belongings were packed, and the Thunderbird was made ready. She had tearfully said goodbye to her close friends and thanked the Gutiérrez family for all of their help. They really did not want her to leave. Severita never had a problem making decisions and she never had a problem following through on her commitments and promises. Going to Mexico to study medicine was her last chance at her dream. She was twenty-six and a single mom.

It took another few weeks to get passports, car papers, vaccination records, school records, and to carefully pack the essentials. The Thunderbird was a large car, but a household of things did not fit. Her mother and father did not want her to go. Her parents and in-laws insisted she leave Kiki with them while she studied in Mexico, but she and Kiki were a team. Wherever she went, Kiki went with her. It was unthinkable to leave him behind. Severita did not even leave their dog, Petunia, behind. After more tearful goodbyes and lots of hugs, Severita took off toward the border.

She crossed into Mexico without incident or delay and within hours was near Monterrey. Severita had traveled this part of Mexico before with Elvira, her mother-in-law. She told Kiki the story of his grandmother Elvira's sad and tragic adventure while crossing into the United States during the Depression years. She and her two brothers, Nicolás and José Olivo, had no choice but to try crossing without proper documents into the United States to find work. They had been starving in Mexico. Little did they know that people in the United States were also starving during the Depression. When they reached the border and attempted to cross the river, others were there also. José, the oldest brother, suggested they wait until dusk to cross. It would be harder for the border patrol to spot them, and perhaps fewer people would be crossing then.

When they got into the river, the three held on to each other with one hand and kept their few belongings high over their heads with the other. Elvira's brothers were very protective of their sister. As they scurried into the brush from the river bank, they heard the border agents, *la migra*, yelling to one another to begin the chase and capture these unwanted people. The three of them were ducking branches and avoiding cactus as they ran deeper into the brush. But they could hear *la migra* on their heels. José pushed Elvira toward the other brother and said, "Go that way. I'll distract them here while you get away."

José started yelling and breaking branches as he led the *Migra* away from the direction of his sister and little brother. Elvira and Nicolás made it deep into the brush as the darkness of the night settled upon them. Fortunately, the moon was full and they could see clearly. They kept walking and walking until exhaustion rendered them helpless. They were out of water and had lost some of their belongings. They made it to nearby Carrizo Springs and waited for José. He had promised to catch up to them as soon as he could. But he never came. After two days of waiting in the hot sun and cool nights without food or water, they had no choice but to go into town and find help.

Elvira never saw her brother again in her lifetime. She only remembered his tortured face as he pushed her away and into the arms of her younger brother. He sacrificed himself so they would have a chance. Worse yet, José had left a wife and child in Saltillo, Mexico. They never saw or heard from him ever again.

Severita told Kiki they were stopping near Saltillo to say hello to Elvira's side of the family.

Elvira's aunts and cousins remembered Severita from when she had last visited with Elvira. It had been a long time. The little nieces and nephews loved the Thunderbird. Severita took them for a ride to the store and gasoline station. The kids made fun of Kiki's Spanish and called him a *pochito*. Kiki was so angry and wanted to leave, but he loved the rides on Uncle Frausto's burro. While the women were talking and preparing a meal, Kiki and the other children played with marbles. Kiki somehow swallowed a large one, which got stuck in his throat. He began to turn purple from the lack of oxygen. Everyone was in a panic, particularly Severita. The prospect of her child dying in Saltillo terrified her.

She grabbed him around the waist, bent him over, and hit him between the shoulder blades. But still Kiki was choking. She hit him harder a third time and out popped the marble. Immediately, Kiki gasped for air and started crying loudly. His color returned. Severita was so relieved and could not wait to leave. In a matter of hours, she, Kiki, and Petunia were on the road to Mexico City.

By nightfall, Severita was straining to stay awake and finally had to stop for sleep. She had been driving for fourteen hours and needed rest. They found a motel by the side of the road on the outskirts of a little town and got a room. The owner suggested she back her car into the parking space by the office so they could keep an eye on it. Severita had so many things in the car and everything was so visible through the windows. The man even suggested she cover up her things with a blanket or sheet, to keep anyone from eyeing the things and getting ideas. She did both things, backed up the car and covered her things. She, Kiki, and Petunia slept soundly until the man knocked on her door early in the morning.

After a quick breakfast and taking an extra order of tacos to go, they hit the road again, going deep into Mexico. The Thunderbird was a great car. It cruised like a magic carpet. Everything worked: the radio, the windows, the air conditioning, the reclining seats, and it hugged the road like Severita did Kiki. Every time they stopped for gas, those nearby would come over to see the car and touch it. Sometimes they would ask questions, and Severita would answer. When too many people crowded around them, Severita would get really nervous and hurry to take off on the road again.

Severita had a CB radio, like the ones the truckers use to communicate with one another. Late the second night while driving in the mountains, she heard them complaining about her. They thought she was a tourist because of the Thunderbird and her driving too slowly. Severita drove slowly because she was scared. And to make things worse, Mexican drivers would flash their headlights on and off as they approached to make sure you saw them coming. Severita would scream each time that happened, and even Petunia would bark. That was so scary.

And sometimes there was no lane line to guide you or shoulder line or barrier, just precipice down the mountain side as the road wound its way around tall peaks.

The truckers would honk at her and come up really, really close behind her, trying to get her to go faster. They had cargo and schedules to keep. They also knew the road, but she didn't. In desperation, she got on the CB radio and began cussing at them. She told them off in Chicano Spanish and pleaded for their understanding of her predicament. She was in a strange country on a horrible road, tired out with a young child—and she could kill them all in a blink is she were not careful. One trucker told her to get to the side of the road at the next bend so that many of the trailers could pass her. He offered to drive behind her and keep others away from her taillights. She saw the straight portion of the road and did as she was told. The truckers zoomed by, one after the other. Some honked as if to say, "Thank goodness!" As she eased back on to the road, another big truck began creeping up behind her again, but at a safe distance. Was it her newfound trucker friend? He confirmed it was over the CB radio. Severita thanked him for the great advice and his protection. They talked about her purpose for going to Mexico City and her dream of becoming a doctor. He complimented her—she was a single mother, older than most students he knew, a Chicana, and going for her dream.

Mexico City was just ahead, but she was running out of gasoline. She told her trucker friend about her need for gas. He warned her not to stop because it was a very bad area with lots of thieves and dangerous, desperate people. The light indicating empty was blinking, she had to stop. It had been blinking for some time, but Severita had just ignored it, because there had not been any gasoline stations along the route. The trucker told her he would not follow her into the next exit; he was late with his cargo.

"Good luck, *seño*. Be very careful."

He signed off and drove on.

Now Severita was really scared. She took the exit anyway. She had no choice. The specter of being stranded on the side of the road near this bad area and out of gas was even worse. She pulled into the first Pemex gasoline station she saw. There were grubby-looking men hanging around. It was predawn. She got out of the car, only to meet an attendant rushing toward her.

Shaking his head, he said, "No, no, no, *señorita*. You should not be here, much less in that car. Those guys over there will attack you. Get out of here."

Severita was in near panic. Kiki wanted to get out. Petunia was barking, also wanting to get out. Some men were giving her the once over, pointing at the car, and nodding to one another. Something was being planned and would soon be coming down.

Severita pleaded with the man to give her gas: "Just a little so I can go up the road."

He agreed. He told her to get back in the car, start the engine, and take off as soon as he hit the trunk with his hand.

"And how do I pay you?" she asked as he pushed her toward the car door.

"Forget it, just get going," he nervously told her. And he began to pump gas into her tank.

Severita saw some of the men begin walking along the driveway toward the side of the road as if to block her exit; others began to walk by the side of the building, as if to encircle her. The attendant hit her trunk loudly, and Severita hit the gas pedal. The T-bird zoomed off as if it had a jet engine. The men jumped out of the way. She made it back onto the freeway with about a quarter tank of gas. She had the pesos in her hand, money she had meant to give the man at the Pemex, but forgot. Her heart was still pounding for miles down the road.

All Severita had was an address in a neighborhood called Churubusco, the same neighborhood where many of the Mexican movies were made. She also had minimal written directions of which roads and exits to take. With every kilometer into the city, the traffic on the freeway got worse, and it was only four in the morning! What were these people doing? Where were they all going? Severita and Kiki had never seen so many cars and people out and about at this hour any place. Then they encountered more trouble: Severita took the wrong exit. She spent a long time trying to get back to the freeway. There were no signs telling her where the freeway was and she had gotten all turned around. She was not very good with directions, and Kiki could not help her.

They made it back and tried again further down the freeway. Now, at the right exit, they hit their first *glorieta*, a circular set of lanes to ease traffic in and out rather than stop at an intersection and wait for the light to change. Traffic on the main boulevards in Mexico City is too congested for traffic lights and stop signs. They use *glorietas* to relieve congestion. Every driver gets on the circle from an outside lane, maneuvers into the center lanes, and moves back out to the outer lane and exits when they get to the opposite side from where they began. It really is a neat way to move traffic from point A to point B without stopping and causing more congestion, but drivers need to be alert and bold, otherwise they will go around and around and around some more. This is what happened to Severita and Kiki. She could not move out in time to get her exit and instead kept going around and around. She was tired. She began to cry. She was afraid to hit another car or be hit. The police might take her car. Then what would they do? In addition, cars were honking, drivers yelling at her and gesturing, and vehicles almost scraping her as they cut her off from one lane or another.

Kiki came to the rescue. He pointed to a police car as they sped around the *glorieta* one more time. Severita went for the cop car, as if by magic, the other cars let her cut them off. She made it back to the outside lane, heading straight for the police car. She didn't realize that this is the method of driving in Mexico City. You get your front half of the car ahead of the other and move in. The other car will let you cut in and out, but you must be bold with nerves of steel as you make your move.

Parked temporarily just ahead of the policeman's car, Severita took a few minutes to compose herself. She could not believe she had done it. She had gotten them off the merry-go-round of a gazillion cars and trucks safely, but she still did not know how to get to the Churubusco address. Severita took too long, and the policeman drove off in hot pursuit of somebody or something.

There was a taxi dropping off a passenger just ahead of them. Severita wasted no time jumping out of the car and running down the street to the taxi. They agreed on a price and the taximan drove them straight to the address on her piece of paper.

The other *becarios* at that address were happy to meet Severita, Kiki, and Petunia. They were surprised at Kiki because the other scholarship students at that address were supposed to be single women. Under the circumstances, Severita got a back set of two tiny rooms, which really were the former maid's quarters. Childcare and school for Kiki posed another set of problems for Severita. At first, the other Chicanas on scholarship helped her out, but they also had to study and attend classes. They were not always available when she needed someone to pick Kiki up from school or feed him. Severita made friends with the lady at a small corner grocery store. Severita paid her to get Kiki from school and keep him at the store until she arrived. Sometimes she fed him too if Severita had late class, laboratory work, or studying to do. Her grocery business was more like a well-stocked pantry than supermarket, but she had the basics for sale and a telephone. The phone was the lifeline for the *becarios*, including Severita and Kiki. Every one of them had gotten sick. Every one of them was homesick. Every one of them had second thoughts about being in Mexico. The Mexican system of doing things was so different and unfriendly to them, they thought.

Some of the professors and many of the Mexican students at the medical school were unkind to the *becarios*. Not all of the *becarios* were studying medicine, like Severita; some were in psychology, economics, art history, and education. But their treatment at the hands of Mexican colleagues and teachers was the same. It seemed as if they resented the Chicano presence in their classrooms and in their country. They made the Chicanos feel unwelcome. Education at public universities in Mexico is practically tuition-free. It is based on merit. Every student can attend any public university and reach for degrees in any field; they just have to pass the very competitive entrance examination. Mexican students and some professors felt that Chicanos were taking spots away from them as well as their tax money. They did not have scholarships. Why should Chicanos? The majority of the people the *becarios* came into contact with were puzzled as to who the Chicanos were. They had never heard about them. Some families had had a member go north in search of work and come back with horrible stories about gringos and Chicano accomplices. The Mexican textbooks that all children read and studied in Mexico did not mention Chicanos, all they included was that the land was lost in the prior century under President Antonio López de Santa Anna.

Kiki took this treatment really hard. One day, he told Severita as she was cooking something for them that he wanted to go home to his dad. Severita did not listen to him or pay close attention to his pain. Kiki bolted out the door and across the patio into the street. He started running as fast as he could. Kiki was too fast for her, so Severita jumped in the car and gave chase. She finally caught up with him and they talked. She drove slowly while he walked. He was crying, and Severita started crying too. She promised him to call Esequiel and ask him if he would come for Kiki. Severita knew that he would not, but to make Kiki return and cope with their new reality in Mexico, she made that promise. Kiki got in the car.

They went to the corner grocery right then and placed the call. In a few minutes, the call went through, but Esequiel refused to accept the call. He was busy at work and would call her back later. Severita explained to his receptionist that he could not just call later because the phone was in a public place and they lived down the block, that he had to talk to Kiki right then. No. He was busy. Esequiel was also hurt that Severita had taken Kiki with her to Mexico. He didn't want him or Severita to leave Crystal City. He had wanted to get back together with Severita. Esequiel did not realize how important Severita's goal of becoming a doctor was to her. He had gotten his degree with her help and had a good-paying job. *His* dreams had come true.

During the *Día de los Muertos* (Day of the Dead) celebrations, the *becarios* had a costume party at the house. They invited other *becarios*, students, teachers, and neighbors. Some of the initial resentment against Chicanos was going away because they refused to be berated and humiliated. They gave history lessons to those who would listen about the Chicano Movement and how most of the *becarios*, if not all, were the children of Mexicans who had gone north in search of work. It was not the Chicanos's fault that they were born in the United States and could not speak Spanish fluently. Why did a lot of Mexicans want to go to the United States even today, the *becarios* would ask their critics.

"Don't you see us as your people? Are we not one people?"

Esequiel arrived at the party unexpectedly. He had flown into Mexico City and taken a taxi to the address given by Severita's parents. Kiki spotted him standing in the patio among all those dancing, singing, and having fun. Esequiel had a disgusted look.

Kiki ran to him and hugged him tightly around his legs. "Papi, Papi . . . Mami, look, Daddy's here. He came for me!" Kiki was shouting over the loud music.

Severita did not hear him.

She was busy dancing with no one in particular, just dancing as she always did, even as a child.

Someone noticed Kiki. The music stopped. Severita saw Esequiel and went to him, but he was angry.

With Kiki hanging onto his waist, he yelled at Severita, "So, this is what you do! Dancing and drinking . . . I bet you have a boyfriend, too. Which one is he?" There were too many questions and all were inappropriate. Severita suggested they go to their room to talk.

Esequiel said no, he had seen enough. He was leaving right then. Kiki tried to hold him back but Esequiel left him standing in the patio, crying his heart out for his daddy.

Severita was heartbroken for her son. The party ended on that sad note. No one had a dry eye.

Severita was not to hear from Esequiel for some time after that incident. Kiki learned to live with the hurt. He learned Spanish really well. Mother and son moved to another house, a bit larger and with more space. The *becarios* staying at this place were married, and it was more family-oriented. They were all in medical school together, which benefited Severita for studying and exams, not to mention after school care for Kiki. Over time, Severita made close friends with the *becarios* as well as with the Mexican students and professors. These friendships came in handy.

Parking at the university campus was a problem. One day Severita parked illegally and came upon her car being towed away. She begged the policeman not to take the car and offered to pay whatever it took, but he refused. The wrecker took off with her T-bird dangling behind. Severita became hysterical. How was she going to get home? Who was going to pick up Kiki from school? What was going to happen to her car? Where was it being taken?

The policeman would not answer her and said, "It's a little late to worry about all that. Why didn't you get your permit? This car is towed and maybe confiscated."

Severita could not believe her ears. She was going to lose the car? The paperwork was wrong? What was wrong? Then it hit her. Her permit for bringing the car into Mexico had expired, and she had failed to renew it.

She begged the policeman to take her to pick up her child and take her home. She offered him money and even to buy him a good dinner at a fancy restaurant. Reluctantly, he agreed. Severita had been making a big spectacle right there in the street, crying, screaming, tearing at her hair, and at the policeman's jacket. He didn't have much of a choice.

Once Kiki and Severita were safely back home, she went to the public phone and called a student friend who was related to the police chief. She also called a professor who put her in touch with an attorney. The attorney managed to find the location of her car and told her he would not be able to help her retrieve the car.

She had lost it. He explained how it was illegal to have a car in Mexico without a permit. Carjacking and car theft were two unpardonable crimes in Mexico. Smugglers would get top dollar, not pesos, for these cars. The new owner would drive around with forged papers and license plates. The police were really cracking down on this racket. They confiscated the cars and sold them at public auction for tax money or just kept them for their own use.

Severita was not about to lose her car. She went to see the relative of the police chief and got to talk to him about her predicament. The police chief promised to retrieve her car, but only gave her three days to leave the country or lose it again forever and go to jail. The police chief told her where to go and who to ask for in order to get her car. Severita wasted no time. She packed her things, gathered up Kiki and Petunia, borrowed money from the other *becarios,* and called Esequiel. He was busy. She called her dad and he promised to wait for her at the border on the Mexican side in Nuevo Laredo. Severita went directly to the designated police station and received her car. The policeman in charge said in Spanish, "I don't know who you are, but you have connections. This T-bird was going to be my car. If I see you anywhere in Mexico, you are mine, and so is your car. We are all going to be on the look out for you."

Severita drove nonstop to the border. She stopped for nothing but gas, tacos, and fruit. Chemita met her as promised and tried his best to dissuade her from renewing the permit and going back. He couldn't.

Severita said, "I *am* going back. I am not quitting my school."

Her dad advised her to take his pickup instead. They would not be looking for her in that. So they traded cars. Chemita slipped her two crisp hundred dollar bills and said, "Here, *mi cabezuda,* take this and be careful."

As fast as she could get a permit for the pickup, she made it back to Mexico City. Severita repaid the money she borrowed and made excuses to her teachers for the classes missed. She visited the relative of the police chief and thanked her profusely.

Then she asked her for another big favor.

"Would you not tell them you have seen me? Just say I got the car and disappeared. Please?"

With promise in hand, Severita moved her living quarters again. She was going to miss her fellow students, but they had to move to avoid the police.

From that day on, Severita was on the look out for policemen. She obeyed all traffic rules and signs, never went past the speed limit and never parked illegally. She also never took the same route to and from school. She placed Kiki in a private school and everything worked out for her—except for one thing.

Kiki got very sick with a stomach infection, and Severita could not care for him and keep up with school. She called Esequiel and begged him to come for Kiki, who was losing weight. He was not eating, and what little he ate, he could not keep down. Esequiel came this time. He and Severita had a good time together while Esequiel rested a couple of days before heading back with Kiki.

Within a month, Severita took the first-class bus from Mexico City to the border and met Esequiel and Kiki. She felt so empty in Mexico without her son and even contemplated leaving her studies to be with him. That weekend at the border was wonderful. The three of them actually got along as a family. It was a new experience. Esequiel asked to her to come home and try again to live like family. She promised to consider it, but went back to her studies and took Kiki back with her.

By Thanksgiving, Severita realized she was pregnant. Esequiel came to visit her during Christmas, and she told Esequiel the good news. He insisted she return to Crystal City. Again, she said no. In disgust, Esequiel returned earlier than he had planned. It was not a happy New Year. It got worse.

Severita came down with a stomach infection that was similar to Kiki's. She self-prescribed medicines to herself and consulted others about her condition. They all agreed it was some powerful strain of amoeba attacking her intestines. Surgery might be necessary if the medicines did not work. They did not work and she continued to waste away day by day, week by week. The baby growing within her was in danger. There were days she was so weak, she hardly could make it to class.

Her doctor told her, "You must go to the United States. Your baby will be born premature and probably die here because we do not have the care such a baby needs. You may also die if you do not get a specialist's care for your stomach problem."

Severita called Esequiel to ask him to come for her, but he was busy and would not take the call. When she did get through to him, he promised to come but never arrived. On three different occasions, she drove to the airport to meet him, only to be disappointed time and again. Money was running low because the medicines she bought for her illness were expensive. Kiki's private school and afterschool care were also costly. What little food she had, she made Kiki eat first.

Other *becarios* saved food for her and gave her what they could. A friend of hers, Mario Salas, insisted she leave the program and save herself and the baby. He urged her to go home and to return once she recovered. He offered to drive her to the border and take the bus back, given that Esequiel was not showing up. Reluctantly, she agreed. He helped her pack everything she had and they gave away to the other *becarios* what she could not fit in the pickup.

Severita called the scholarships's office and told them she had to quit the program, but requested that her slot be held until returned. She called home and asked Chemita to meet her at the border, just like before. What normally would take about a day nonstop took two days to reach the border at Laredo. They had to stop often because of Severita's diarrhea. Severita was in bad shape and getting worse.

While still on the Mexican side by the bus station, Kiki started yelling, "Papi, Papi. Look, Mami—it's Papi."

Severita looked and saw this dirty, rumpled man with messy hair slowly walking down the street. He looked like a homeless person.

"No, Kiki, be quiet," she admonished Kiki.

"Yes, yes, it's him," he yelled and managed to open the door and leap out. He ran toward his father and hugged him around the waist. The man looked down and up and around in amazement. It was Esequiel.

When things calmed down and Mario had left them to catch his bus, Esequiel explained he had flown to Mexico City and gone to her apartment. She was gone, they told him. Being without enough money to catch a plane back, he had taken a bus. He had not eaten in days because he had no money.

Esequiel got Severita across the border, found her father, and they all made it back to Crystal City that February 1980. Severita was taken into emergency care and was in intensive care for days until she was rehydrated. The doctors told her the prognosis by her Mexican doctor was correct. She was lucky to be alive, and the baby was going to be born premature. All they could hope for was that it would be healthy, given her condition of deprivation and malnutrition. The Lara family, the de La Fuente family, and all who knew of her condition prayed for divine intervention. Severita was transported to Eagle Pass for the delivery.

On March 25, 1980, her premature baby was born, another boy. She named him Eli. He was tiny, anemic, and could not breathe on his own. The doctors flew him to San Antonio for emergency care. Severita was given massive dosages of antibiotics, now that she was no longer pregnant, and began to respond well to the medication. She insisted on being with her baby in San Antonio and left the hospital in Eagle Pass against her doctor's orders. In San Antonio, she slept on the floor in Eli's room. The stitches from her Caesarean section ripped open, but she was determined to breast-feed Eli to make him stronger. This ordeal continued for a month until Eli was out of danger. When she took him home to Crystal City, he was so small, he fit in a shoe box. Severita bought male dolls and used their clothes for him.

Severita moved into the trailer Esequiel lived in and continued to nurse the baby. She in turn was cared for by Kiki when he came home from school. He was now ten years old. Severita had no money and was totally dependent on Esequiel, but he had developed a serious drinking problem. Seldom did he come home sober or give her money. He never bought groceries. Kiki convinced the neighborhood convenience store owner, Mr. Múzquiz, to let him take food, but charge it as beer on his dad's credit account.

After the baby was bigger and Severita stronger, she moved out of the trailer and found a job. She began to climb out of debt and make a home for Kiki and Eli. Her parents helped, as did her in-laws, but not Esequiel. What hopes she had for reconciliation and making a family with him were dashed once again. And now she had to forget about her dream of becoming a doctor. With two children and suffering from ill health herself, she was not going to go back and finish. The scholarships's office and university wrote to her several times, urging her to return, offering her the scholarship, but she declined. She knew that this time she would be taking the opportunity away from someone else.

Chapter 7
Here Comes the Judge

After caring for Eli the first two years of his life, Severita took a job with Winter Garden Hospital in Crystal City. She became the x-ray and laboratory technician. She was so good that a doctor offered to bring her into the business if she would get her certifications. Severita did not take up his offer because she really wanted to get out of Crystal City and start a new life with her sons. Severita decided to leave town and make more money. A friend, Rosalinda Treviño, offered her housing in Dallas if she moved there. That's what she did and found a great paying job with Warner Cable. Within months, Severita was earning more money than she ever dreamed possible. And Dallas was big and exciting. For a while during this time, Severita thought she was going to spend her life in Dallas, Texas, raising her sons by herself, and maybe meet someone else and marry later on. But it was not to be.

Chemita had been ill for years and had a second stroke and a heart attack. He needed constant care. Severita's life in Dallas came to an abrupt end. She hurried back to Crystal City to stay to help care for her dad. Her life now revolved around Eli, her teenage son Kiki, her dad, and the stormy relationship with Esequiel, the father of her sons. They tried living together again and even going into business together. Since her dad had his crippling strokes, the gas station had been replaced by a small store. The store was not more than a ten-foot-by-ten-foot box; it mainly sold beer to go. The problem was that more beer went out the back door for Esequiel and his buddies than out the front door for cash.

Severita gave up on that business and Esequiel again. She next found a job with the local school board, which was apprehensive about hiring her. She was the walkout leader who could easily lead current students to walk out again. She still had fire in the belly, the talk that motivated people, and the political courage to speak her mind anywhere. She proved that when a local teacher had molested children. Severita led the protests for his immediate removal and subsequent criminal trial. She also demanded that the school authorities be held liable for their gross negligence in not investigating the early reports about the teacher and his sexual attacks on classroom children in his care. Severita was feared because she was effective and brave.

She also worked as a fifth-grade teacher and was under regular surveillance by administrators and school board members. They were always on the look out for any early signs of her political involvement with students. One day, she was summoned to explain why she was teaching the kids radical songs. They were singing "Yo Soy Chicano" ("I Am Chicano"). Things had really changed in Crystal City from the heyday of the Chicano Civil Rights movement and La Raza Unida Party in the early 1970s. Everything was much more conservative now. The next year, the school board reassigned her to the high school to teach biology and other science courses. Ten years later, she was made a librarian, away from students and hidden in the book stacks.

By 1986, Severita was disgusted with the politics in Crystal City. Everything was back to what it had been before the walkout. The only difference was that now there were brown Hispanic faces sitting behind the desks and with the titles the Anglos had had before them. People complained of the lack of street repair, the dearth of programs and jobs, police brutality, and rising drug-related crime. The old-time activists from Ciudadanos Unidos, while they did not meet on Sundays anymore, did meet with one another and would reminisce. They regularly complained of the current county judge, an Anglo-American, Ronnie Carr, who had been appointed by an all-Mexican commisioner's court. They had not even considered one another or any other Chicano; they appointed the only Anglo officeholder in the courthouse. Severita was encouraged to seek that position. She could win, they told her. People would rally behind her like they had before. She was still their leader.

After discussing the possible political campaign with Esequiel and her family, she made up her mind to challenge Ronnie Carr. He was up for reelection in 1986. The old network of La Raza Unida Party voters and Ciudadanos Unidos members was revived. They came out of the woodwork to volunteer for her campaign. They had a candidate of their own and a cause once again. Hundreds of people would show up at rallies, where Severita spoke and asked for their votes. They registered voters. They cooked and prepared thousands of barbecued chicken plates. Money was raised, but not enough. The price of printing and radio advertisements had more than doubled since the 1970s. To avoid paying an expensive filing fee to the Democratic Party to have her name on the ballot, she chose to gather signatures instead, an alternative method to file for office.

Severita and her volunteers started walking the streets, block by block, talking to registered voters. Her early experience with door knocking during the 1970 school and city elections really came in handy. Everyone in her campaign with prior membership in Ciudadanos Unidos knew exactly what to do. Her campaign was a well-oiled machine. Esequiel devoted all his time to her campaign, serving as her campaign manager. He was an experienced political worker, having been involved with the La Raza Unida Party in many, many elections.

The campaign volunteers all worked well together and the effort went smoothly, except for money. She needed more money to fight against the negative radio advertising campaign coming from her opponent. He had money, plenty of it. He had ads on several radio stations. Every other day, he leveled a new charge, accusation, allegation, rumor, or nasty comment about her and the former La Raza Unida Party. Their Chicano political party had been decertified back in 1978, when the gubernatorial candidate, Mario Compeán, did not get sufficient votes to remain on the ballot. In addition, state legislature, which regulates political parties in the state, also raised the minimum percentage of votes to twenty percent the prior year for a political party to remain on the ballot.

Severita huddled with her supporters and backers about the need for more campaign funds. A major leader of Ciudadanos Unidos and former school board president, José O. Mata, and his wife, Beatriz, came to her rescue. They agreed to cosign for a bank loan from the local Zavala County Bank. Severita borrowed $7,000. With that money, the fund-raising could continue and help pay off the loan, but cash could now be used to buy more radio spots, print more sample ballots, and reimburse volunteers for the gasoline consumed in traveling the entire county.

Outside of Crystal City, people in the county knew of her, but did not *know* her. Besides, a woman running for this position was threatening to some Chicano male voters. The county judge was the one that tried cases involving driving while intoxicated as well as cases for nonpayment of child support, as had been the case with Esequiel, her former husband. In fact, Esequiel had to go among the men and assure them that she was not out to get them anymore than Judge Carr had been. He promised that Severita as judge would simply enforce the law and be reasonable with everyone. She understood that some men could not pay if they had no job or only seasonal work.

This specific issue was problematic for Severita. The fact that she was a woman running for the top position did not bother anyone. Crystal City and Zavala County voters had long been used to female political leaders, such as Virginia Múzquiz, Enriqueta Palacios, Elvirita de la Fuente, Gregoria Delgado, and Elena Díaz. Not many Chicanas had ever run for county judge, and only one had been elected in the entire state: Alicia Chacón in El Paso.

The real problem was in running a strategic campaign. There were three strong candidates in the race for county judge: Ronnie

Carr, Justice of the Peace Eliseo Sánchez, and Severita. The first part tactic was to ensure Severita was either the top vote getter or the second. If no candidate received a majority of the votes cast, another election had to be held, a runoff election between the top two vote getters. Severita and her supporters had to be careful not to offend those who might support Eliseo Sánchez, because they would need his supporters in case of a runoff. The second tactic was to carefully budget for the campaign. Her supporters were all poor people, mostly seasonal agricultural workers with little money. The strategy was to stay in the race to the end and win by getting out her voters, possibly twice, if a primary runoff was necessary. Since there would be no Republican opponent in the November general election, victory was hers either in May or in the runoff in June, thirty days after the primary election.

First, they had to motivate to action those persons who preferred to vote early during the absentee voting period, which began twenty days before election day on May 7. Voters eligible to vote early were the elderly, the sick, and those not present on election day because they were in the military, away at college, or working out of the county that day, including truckers and migrant workers up north. From the list of those registered voters, Severita and her campaign crew sought out addresses and mailed applications requesting a ballot for those not in the county. They visited the elderly and the sick who were physically unable to go to the polls and helped them either go to the county clerk's office to vote early or be taken by car on election day so that the election judge could come outside with a ballot for them to vote in their car. Telephone calls, sometimes over long distance, were made to those outside the county, encouraging them to send in their applications and return ballots in the mail on time for the counting of all votes on election day. Severita had to find poll watchers, volunteers to monitor the voting at the county clerk's office during those first twenty days and on election day too in order to make sure no cheating went on and that all her votes were counted correctly. The election was going to be won one vote at a time, day by day.

Then election day was upon them. The absentee period was over. The major effort now was to get all volunteers to put up her political advertisement signs by the polling places all over the county and begin knocking on doors to get voters out on election day. The weekend before the election, a night rally had been held at La Plazita, the same place that Los Cinco Candidatos and the La Raza Unida Party always held their rallies. Severita's speeches at all rallies and radio spots hit Judge Carr hard on his lack of government spending on Chicano needs as well as his favoritism in hiring workers in the county programs and offices. She attacked him for never being in the office and for his leniency in sentencing drug offenders. The Friday night before election day, a giant rally was held at Juan García Park. The rally was a huge success, and Severita's speech was very well received by the audience. The general feeling was that she would win.

On election day, her volunteers trying to get people to vote crisscrossed every street in the towns across the county, concentrating on Crystal City, where the majority of voters resided. Others were calling people by telephone, urging the same thing: Go vote for Severita, now! It was a Saturday and people were doing laundry and housework, buying groceries, paying bills, and the things they usually did on weekends. Some voters were annoyed at the knocking on their doors and the telephone calls; others were not home; and still others said they would go later. Women at home usually said they would go vote when their husbands came home. These "go later" people were key because the polls closed at 7 p.m.

When the polls closed, Severita and her supporters gathered at the courthouse to hear the results announced and see them posted on the giant board she had put up for all to read. Slowly, the votes were posted on the giant board. Judge Carr got the majority of the absentee votes. Many voters, mostly Chicanos, voted for him because they had a case pending in his court or they had promised him their vote for some other favor. Severita trailed, with Sánchez close behind her. It looked like a runoff election was going to be necessary. The votes came in from area cities, and Severita jumped ahead in the count. Into the night, the vote count seesawed back and forth between her and Judge Carr. Eliseo Sánchez was still in the race, however, within a few votes from both her and Carr. Then around 10 p.m., it was over. No one candidate had a majority of the votes cast. Judge Carr had the most votes, with Severita right behind him. Eliseo Sánchez was twelve votes behind Severita. It was a very, very close election. She was headed for a runoff election with Judge Carr.

Severita's campaign crew and volunteers had a celebration, but not a big one. They had plenty of work ahead and had to start the runoff campaign as soon as possible. Everything had to be repeated. Absentee applications and votes had to be gotten all over again. The radio spots had to be changed from the last round of advertisements to thanking the voters and asking them to vote again for her in the runoff. The campaign resumed knocking on doors and making phone calls the following Monday. They held more rallies. New sample ballots were printed to show people how the ballot would look and how to vote for her. (Voters could not get someone to help them mark their ballots at the polling place unless they were blind or physically handicapped and could not mark the ballots.)

Her closest advisors suggested she seek out Eliseo Sánchez to see if he would endorse her and ask his supporters to vote for her instead of Judge Carr. He was very upset at having lost by a mere twelve votes and would not commit to an endorsement of her campaign. And to make matters worse, another set of candidates was locked into a runoff also. Each group had its own campaign, and voters could make mistakes in voting in only one race and not the other involving Severita. She was also running out of money. More barbecue chicken plates were made and sold.

Again, the campaign made an effort to get early voters into the county clerk's office to vote, and recruited poll watchers to watch the balloting on election day. Food had to be prepared and delivered to the poll watchers, because they were not allowed to leave the polling place until the election was over at 7 p.m.

The last rally was held Friday evening before the election, and Severita shined in her speech. She was so eloquent. She was a gutsy fighter. She mentioned how some people had approached her to drop out of the race. She told the audience she had a witness to the bribery attempt.

"But I'm not for sale. I prefer to lose than have that on my conscience," she told the wildly cheering crowd.

Severita did not give names regarding this attempted bribe. Her attack on Judge Carr was focused on issues, not on personal matters.

Severita barely won the runoff. She received one more vote than Carr. Her campaign workers had outworked Carr's. Everyone was jubilant at the squeaker of a victory, but soon they realized this election was headed for the courthouse. Judge Carr immediately announced he wanted a recount of votes. And he personally went out to ask people to serve on the recount committee, something he could not legally do. This was a blatant conflict of interest; he was the candidate, even if he was the chief election officer by title as county judge.

Judge Carr named Daniel Díaz as the chairman of the committee, along with Mariana Tapia and Margot Garza López as members. The three of them were his supporters. Only after Severita complained to the Democratic Party county chairman about how the committee was stacked with Carr supporters was she allowed to name her friend María Torres as her lone representative on the recount. All the seasoned veterans from the La Raza Unida Party advised Severita to hire a lawyer; they sensed treason by the recount committee in the making.

Chairman Daniel Díaz did his dirty work the day of the recount. He eliminated one vote for Severita, claiming it was a mutilated ballot and invalid. A voter had scratched out Ronnie Carr's name and put a mark by her name, indicating Severita was the choice. Now the count was tied, since Severita had won by only one vote. Then, Díaz declared a vote previously counted for

Severita as really being for Carr because the voter mark was closer to his name than hers. It was not. María Torres protested loudly, but she was outvoted by the others. Now Carr led by one vote.
Díaz threw out another of Severita's votes with another silly argument. Carr was declared the winner by two votes. Judge Carr was
reelected.

José O. and Beatriz Mata, along with many others, insisted
that Severita contest the election, get the result of the recount
committee thrown out, and have her victory upheld. San Antonio
attorney Randolph Janssen, whom Esequiel worked for, would
help. Severita's campaign volunteers immediately began a new
round of fund-raising, mostly by personal solicitation for cash
donations. Court cases are expensive and this one might even
take an appeal before it would be settled. People handed Severita dollar bills, a five here, a ten there, and an occasional twenty.

Attorney Janssen filed his pleadings for a contested election.
He had never done one before, but was willing to try and would
not charge Severita a penny. He too was incensed at the under-
handednes of Chairman Díaz and the appointed committee. A
visiting district judge was appointed because a local judge might
not be impartial. But everyone knew from the La Raza Unida
Party days and the Cinco Candidatos era that every time an outside judge sat on an election contest case in Crystal City, they
ruled against Mexican American candidates.

The case was set for a preliminary hearing. The courtroom
itself was packed with Severita's supporters, and the crowd
spilled into the hallways and even outside the building. Judge
Carr was there with his attorney and Severita with hers. After the
visiting district judge took his seat and called the case, Janssen
rose to begin his opening argument about the recount committee.
The judge interrupted him and asked why the petition had not
been filed earlier before the canvass of votes by the commission-
er's court. Randolph Janssen tried to explain that Judge Carr as
county judge had hurried up that process and further, that he had
a conflict of interest. The visiting judge asked Janssen why he had

not stopped that process with an injunction. It was clear to all listening that Carr did not need to have an attorney present, because the visiting judge was doing all the arguing against Severita's case. The visiting judge cut off Janssen's presentation with the announcement that the election contest was late in being filed and he would not hear the substantive matter of the recount committee and the vote tallies. He dismissed her case.

When Severita attempted to speak, the judge just said, "If you disagree with my ruling, take me up on appeal." With that he banged the gavel and stepped down from the bench.

The Chicano audience was stunned. They began to boo and shout. It was of no use—the judge had made a decision.

Severita was crying and asking over and over, "Why? Why? It is not fair. How can he do this? Why? What are we going to do?"

Janssen lead her outside and into his car, with Esequiel right behind them.

The people outside were shouting questions in her direction. "What happened? Did we win?" Others pointed out, "Look, something happened. Severita is crying." José O. Mata caught up with them as they were to drive off and asked them to meet immediately at his house down the street, just blocks from the courthouse. A few more people showed up at the Mata residence. Beatriz started making coffee and clearing the dining table.

Inside the Matas' house, Severita was still crying and in shock over the antics of the visiting judge. She could not believe the election victory had been stolen from her by Carr's cronies and was now being confirmed by the visiting judge right in front of her. He had not even let them talk about the case, just shut them down. It was as if he also was sent down to Crystal City to finish the hatchet job on her candidacy. There would be no Chicana county judge in Zavala County.

José O. and Beatriz Mata were pros at politics. Beatriz was one of the best campaign workers in town. She knew more people than anyone, and people trusted her. José, a Vietnam veteran, had been a leader from the day he returned from the service, right after the walkout. He had held public office in the recent past and knew what questions to ask of Janssen.

"How much is it going to cost for the appeal?" he asked.

Janssen had never done an election contest, much less an appeal of one, so he responded cautiously and nervously. "I think the transcript will be about a thousand or two, plus the filing fees, and maybe a bond is required. I really don't know right this minute. Five thousand is my quick guess."

Those gathered gasped at the amount. Five thousand dollars was a lot of money.

José was not shocked at the figure. He followed up with: "By when do you need to file the appeal?"

José knew that answer would determine if Severita could fight the decision or not. The deadline for filing was the real deadline for raising the money, regardless of how much it was.

The group of supporters at the Mata house left quickly, but only after assuring Severita that they would fight alongside her and raise the money somehow. Beatriz and José also bid her, Esequiel, and Janssen farewell.

"We're with you, Severita. Hang in there," José advised.

It was not a question of quitting or not. It was a question of affordability. Carr had the entire backing of the Anglo Democratic Party, the judges, and the public office he held. He had money and access to more than Severita could ever match. He simply could outspend, outlast, and outfight her in court. Janssen was too new and inexperienced. A well-seasoned attorney would cost her even more than five thousand dollars, on top of the five or so thousand of court costs. She still owed the seven thousand dollars at the local bank. Her decision would ultimately hinge on a risk, a very huge gamble. Would she win in court, eventually, and also be able to pay off the expensive litigation costs?

Severita and Esequiel had a heart-to-heart talk that night, as did José and Beatriz Mata. The Matas reached a decision to pay off Severita's debt. They had cosigned the loan, but could not afford to give her any more money for the court battle. Severita and Esequiel reached the same decision. They could not afford to fight. The existing debt would take the two of them several years to pay off. But more importantly, Severita felt she could not ask her supporters, all very poor people, to give her more money. And Carr would remain in office until midnight of December 31, 1986, five long months in which to harshly punish poor people standing before him in court, should he lose the judgeship. It was a time to cut their losses and give up the fight. They had run a great race, the people had supported and voted for her, and they had done it cleanly, honestly, morally, and in good faith. Everyone knew she had won and had had the election stolen from her.

Severita called José O. Mata with her decision. She called Randall Janssen next. He was still in San Antonio researching how to do the appeal and how much it would cost. Before she could tell him to drop the case, he informed her that a supersedeas bond would be required, which was two times the annual salary for the elected office. He calculated that to be about $60,000. It did not need to be in cash, but could come from people with property signing it over until the case ended.

Severita was numb with the figures he was spouting and finally interrupted him. "I'm not going to fight it. Leave it be. We do not have the money. Thank you. I'll see you when you come to Crystal City to thank you in person."

She hung up the telephone and cried quietly. She was not in pain nor hurt. She was disappointed to her inner core, that justice was not available for poor people. Political power was not in the hands of those who voted; it was in the hands of those who counted the votes and decided the court cases. It was not fair or democratic or about justice. It was all about the powerful and the powerless.

She decided to quit politics and concentrate on her family. She had bills to pay.

Severita made one last effort that took a lot of resolve. She went to the radio station and bought three radio spots with the last cash she had. She thanked the public for their votes and closed with, "I know how to lose. This election was not lost; it was stolen. Tomorrow will be another day. May God bless you all."

Judge Carr was incensed at her farewell announcement. He searched for any way to sue her and found a campaign reporting violation. Severita had failed to file the last report of her contributions and expenditures. Attorney Janssen paid her fine because it would cost more to defend the charge in court.

Severita left politics. Even leaders get tired of the fight sometimes. Many candidates fail to file campaign reports but seldom are charged with a crime, much less made to pay a fine.

Years later, when Daniel Díaz was ill, he asked Severita for forgiveness. He knew he had done her wrong. He even admitted to her that it was all for money, a measly $1,500. Severita forgave him.

Judge Carr went on to run for a higher judicial office and won. He retired with an ample pension and became a visiting judge.

Chapter 8
Mayor Severita Lara

When the county judge position was open again in 1990 because Ronnie Carr was seeking a seat on the area appellate court, Severita watched others run. She stayed home. She continued teaching and tending to the books at the library. She watched her sons grow into young men. Things were the same between her and Esequiel. She grew accustomed to his ways and shortcomings. She still loved him, in spite of all his flaws. They lived together as a family. Kiki went off to the University of Wisconsin in Madison, but came back homesick after just one semester. He claimed it was too cold and that he missed her and his brother.

Eli, thin and tall, was fourteen when the county judge position was up once again in 1994. His premature birth was but a memory. Severita was thinking about making the race one more time. Politics were in her blood and soul. Politics gets you positions with which to make policy for the people's welfare. It also lets a public official spend money in budgets to make the lives of people easier.

After the stolen election, from 1986 to 1993, Severita had watched Crystal City deteriorate from what it had been in the 1970s, right after the walkout she had led. The loss of programs and jobs in the city was epidemic. A few families controlled all the jobs and opportunities. Not a single new program had been initiated, and the programs started back then were gone. Taxes were the highest in the area. Local officeholders, when they lost programs, raised taxes to maintain funding levels and their salaries. Drugs were a serious problem in the city. The youth in the city had absolutely no recreation facilities. They were dropping out of school like flies. The few Chicanos that went to college were those whose parents had benefited from the walkout and the subsequent programs begun by La Raza Unida Party. The city streets were in deplorable condition, in desperate need of paving—potholes were everywhere. The roads in the outlying cities of La Pryor and Batesville that Raza Unida officeholders in the county had paved for the first time in history were completely in disrepair. The vicious cycle of poverty was back in place. With insufficient jobs, welfare rolls swelled. The health care programs started by Raza Unida leaders were now controlled by a select few. Many Mexican Americans talked badly about that time in history, as if to run away from the civil rights struggle. Severita continued to embrace the movement that had uplifted the Chicano community in Crystal City. She was disgusted with the quality of life in her hometown and wanted to do something about it.

The debt from the 1986 election had taken her three years to pay off. She had made a payment of $189 a month to retire that debt. She drove a used car and passed up buying new things as she struggled to pay for Kiki's college and Eli's teenage needs. Esequiel worked but she seldom could count on his contribution. She paid for everything required by the family. Her dad remained wheelchair-bound and sickly. He had gotten back some of his movement and speech, but it was very slurred; only close family members could understand him. Chemita would cry when he struggled with words that never came out of his mouth and movements he could not make. Severita spent a great deal of time with him.

During the Christmas holidays of 1992, Severita conferred with the Matas and others about the possibility of running for the city council. José O. Mata had run for that post, won, and served. He encouraged her and was glad she was interested. He also warned her that it was very time-consuming and often a headache because people constantly came to council members with complaints; however, it was only the city manager who could make the day-to-day decisions.

In 1993, Severita filed to run for city council and began her campaign. She knew what to do. She promised Esequiel and her family that she would not get into debt during this race. If people wanted her in office, they had to vote for her. They knew who she was and what she believed in. There was no need for an elaborate and expensive campaign. She carefully selected her campaign volunteers and was precise in guiding their efforts. This time, she held no public rallies, sold no barbecue plates, and organized no large numbers of volunteers to knock on doors or make phone calls. She did most of the campaigning herself, starting early with visits to homes of ardent supporters from years past to ask them for their vote. Chicano families in Crystal City had extended families; everyone was related by blood or marriage to dozens of others. She asked each person she spoke with to recruit their neighbors for her. In this way, a network of supporters began to form around her candidacy.

At quiet backyard cookouts, she raised some money for sample ballots and gasoline. She paid for a few printed advertisements in the local newspaper rather than spend a lot of money she did not have on radio commercials. She ran on her own even though others were running at the same time and could be her opponents. Unlike the county race where the person with a majority of the vote won in either a primary or runoff election, a city race was won by the top vote getters.

Crystal City voters knew Severita and gave her their votes. She was still their voice and their leader. She won a seat on the city council. Her swearing in ceremony was a joyous affair. Her sons and Esequiel were there beaming with pride. Her dad got to see her elected to public office. Her mother was proud of her, as were her sisters and their husbands.

Severita became knowledgeable about municipal affairs, including taxation, zoning, the municipal court, the police, governmental relations with the state and federal government. She took an interest in the city library, long neglected but something she knew a lot about as a biology teacher in the public schools. She went to meetings with other city officials from neighboring communities and learned from them. She began to understand the transformation that had taken place from the 1970s to the 1990s.

Computers were now the big thing. Everything was being computerized and jobs were lost in the process. Agriculture was a thing of the past—farmers and ranchers were leasing their lands for hunting and to the government rather than growing crops and raising cattle. Del Monte, the local food processing plant, had been downsized and had but a skeleton crew working on making juice from concentrate rather than packing vegetables. The entire rural economy was in a tailspin. There was more need than jobs; more demand for services and less tax revenue; fewer skilled workers and more demand for computer-literate employees. A small town could only support those who worked for the local government and for small businesses. The local governments, the city, the schools, and the county were now the largest employers of people. A job in those institutions was the lifeline for survival. Most people just moved away from Crystal City; there was no future in staying. But some people could not move out.

Severita made it her mission while on the council to improve the quality of life as best she could for those who stayed in Crystal City. She pushed for more programs, paving of streets, and books in the library. She sought to prevent the police from hurting people, lowered taxes, and provided housing for the elderly. She tried and tried and learned and learned. City managers came and went. It was a real headache and consumed a lot of time, as José O. Mata had warned her it would be.

She spent many nights pouring over reports and budgets, trying to find monies to accomplish the initiatives that would benefit her people.

Severita served two terms of two years each on the city council. Her reelection in 1995 went without a hitch because she ran unopposed. During her years on the city council, she served with María Rivera, who was the mayor. María and Severita got along well on the council. The biggest decisions and conflicts arose between them and the other council members over the police and the firing and hiring of the city manager.

The real power in city government rested with the city manager. He was the one to hire and fire almost all the city employees. In order for the council members to make changes in the operation of the city or its personnel, they had to fire the city manager and find one who agreed with the overall objectives of the majority of council members. Severita's brother-in-law, Ramón de la Fuente, had been a city manager in Crystal City and she sought him out for advice from time to time. She also voted to fire him when he refused to implement the policies voted upon by the city council. During the time Severita was on the city council, Crystal City went through five city managers.

Because there were five members of the city council, including the mayor, the only way to get something done was either to be friends with the city manager or have three votes to make a motion at a regular meeting and change policy. In Severita's second term, the police became an issue with city residents. The drug traffic in the city was out of control. The police hired an undercover officer, but made no arrests. The bills from the police department kept growing, yet the force produced no results. It seemed as if the undercover policeman was traveling everywhere with a city credit card. The police chief refused to give an accounting or explanation for these questionable expenditures. The city manager seemed unconcerned, but Mayor Rivera was adamant about cutting back on this drain on the budget. Severita shared her concern, but they were one vote shy. No one else on the council wanted to take up that issue. The problem only got worse.

Finally, the budget hearings came around for the next fiscal year. Severita pushed for the position of undercover policeman to be eliminated from the budget. The city manager refused to remove the line item. Word got out and into the newspaper about the conflict between the police department and the city council, particularly about Severita and Mayor Rivera's concerns. Severita started to get threatening phone calls late at night. She changed her phone number. The members of the police department started attending all hearings and stood menacingly in the crowd. Over the next few meetings, more law enforcement officials from the constables to the sheriff's office and Texas Department of Public Safety, or Highway Patrol, also began to stand around during city council meetings.

At an open regular meeting of the city council, Severita made a motion to adopt the budget as recommended by the city manager but without the line item for the undercover agent. The council hall fell silent. It was as if she had called for the world to end. This time the entire police force, the county, and the Highway Patrol were in attendance, sitting in the front three rows. No other council member seconded Severita's motion. The mayor looked at each member for a clue as to their possible vote. She then seconded Severita's motion. The matter was now up for discussion. The police chief asked to speak and proceeded to accuse the council members, the mayor, and Severita specifically about not wanting to fight drugs in the city. He insisted he needed that position to combat crime. Others given permission to speak, even though they were not council members, pointed out that the city manager ran the city and he knew best what to recommend; that was why the undercover agent's position was included.

The meeting got tense. The mayor called for the vote. More silence. She repeated the call for the vote with a show of hands in favor. Finally, a third member raised his hand. The budget motion passed with the amendment to drop the undercover agent. The police, as if on cue, got to their feet together and walked out of the meeting. The city manager grabbed his papers and stormed out, saying, "Run the city any way you want. I'm not putting up with this."

The Sentinel, the local newspaper, ran that story as headline news. The city manager resigned. The police chief threatened to resign. The mayor was threatened with a recall election, and the city council was badly divided. Eliseo Sánchez, the third-place finisher in the 1986 county judge election, was on the council in the camp backing the police and city manager. Severita and María were in the other camp. In the subsequent city council elections, María Rivera was defeated and new members came into office: Jesse Guerrero and Bernard Leeper, the Anglo banker. Crystal City had not had an Anglo on the city council since 1970. The council meeting was packed with relatives and friends of the newly elected. The chamber was standing room only.

A first order of business after the swearing in of new members usually is the selection of mayor from within the council members. Councilman Sánchez, Severita's nemesis, nominated Juan Hernández for mayor. There was no other visible support for his nomination. Nobody nodded his head in agreement or gave any hint of encouragement. Freshman councilman Leeper then nominated Severita for mayor. Jesse Guerrero, the other freshman, said, "I second the nomination," even though it was not necessary to second a nomination; only a motion requires a second.

Everyone could sense that with two public statements made in favor of Severita, surely she would vote for herself for mayor. That added up to three votes out of five, a majority. Sánchez and Hernández nodded. They saw defeat in the making and went ahead to make the nomination by acclamation, unanimous. Thunderous applause rang out like confetti on New Year's Eve. Severita was the mayor. People rushed over to hug her and congratulate her. She could not conduct the meeting with such pandemonium. To his credit, Councilman Sánchez moved for the meeting to adjourn and four hands went up. The congratulatory celebration around Severita really got going. People forgot about Leeper and Guerrero. Sánchez and Hernández quietly slipped out and away from the meeting. It was Severita's night.

The major business that started her term of office was the selection of a new city manager. The council hired Miguel Delgado, brother to the new owner of the local newspaper. He was very conservative and not a risk taker, very much a slow, methodical manager. He and Severita locked horns right away over a mural to be painted on the outer wall of the library, depicting the Chicano history of struggle. The mural was one of the grant projects she had worked on and obtained funding for as a council member. Severita wanted the walkout scene at the center of the mural. Delgado was not in favor. Severita wanted a scene of the Japanese concentration camp that operated in Crystal City during World War II. Americans of Japanese ancestry were arrested and jailed in this camp and others across the country on suspicion that they would help Japan. Busloads of Japanese Americans, descendants of those interned in the camp, would come annually to Crystal City to see the area and its monument. Severita thought erecting a monument was particularly important because the buildings of the concentration camp had long been demolished. Delgado thought this was too political. Severita wanted the image of the Spinach Festival Queen removed and a voter registration table with people filling out forms included. Delgado opposed that also. The queen image was removed, but the voter registration table was not included.

Mayor Lara got into more political hot water over appointments. She attempted to replace the police chief with another, but failed to get the votes. In the housing authority, an agency of the city, several members were habitually absent from meetings. Severita removed them and appointed others. These appointments caused her grief when the fired workers sued. The housing authority scandal grew into lawsuits on top of lawsuits. Diana Palacios was removed as executive director and Ana María Farías named in her place by the new commissioners appointed by Mayor Lara. Ms. Farías had been a high official during the George H.W. Bush administration. Rumors began circulating that Severita was now a Republican. Councilman Leeper was a Republican and he was in her political corner.

Ex-mayor María Rivera began a recall petition against Severita and almost succeeded in getting the sufficient number of signatures for an election. Though the recall did not work, opposing it took valuable time and effort on Severita's part. Severita also had to take on the cable television provider with the exclusive franchise in Crystal City. People complained constantly to her as mayor about the bad service and reception, plus increasing monthly costs. Severita tried to get the city manager to hold the cable company operator's feet to the fire on the terms of the contract. He was not interested and never did much. She finally called them to a meeting herself. She scolded them for the bad service and mentioned her own classroom experience in the high school with poor cable reception and service. They fixed it the next day. Severita learned to use the power of her office, but also learned the negatives that come from using that power. There is always opposition from someone.

As mayor, she had new housing created for the elderly, trees planted at La Placita, and streets repaired. But she only remained at the helm for one year. It was too much. Now at age 45 and in the last year of her second term on the council, she tired easily. The stress level from frustration at not moving things along at a faster pace constantly was a concern. Her health was poor. Too many meetings well into the night consumed her evenings. City council membership was unpaid, so work at school had to continue.

Her dream of building a youth recreational center was not becoming a reality. The first planning grant was just being sought. The city manager could make things happen and also keep things from happening. The police continued to be criticized for brutal treatment of the citizenry. Severita had to investigate matters herself and make the police answer questions about incidents. She lost friends and fellow activists from the past, such as Diana Palacios, Jesse Gámez, Rudy Torres, and Estelita Andrade. The latter two she removed from the housing authority, and they became her political enemies. Others just quit being involved. The rumor mill was never ending. Stories in the local newspaper and on the radio about city business demanded explanations. She was asked about this and that at the grocery store, at the movie rental, at the pizza place, everywhere she went. It was too much.

Severita Lara did not seek reelection or any other public office after her term as mayor. Even so, Severita has retired before, only to come back and fight again. Only time will tell if she will return to political work again. In the mean time, her legend is clear: Severita Lara was the Chicana student leader from the 1960s who rose to become the mayor of her hometown.

Epilogue

This book ends in the late 1990s with Severita Lara's term as mayor of Crystal City, Texas, but life has continued. First, Severita, disillusioned with Democratic Party politics, has become a member of the Republican Party. Second, she returned to college and obtained another degree, a Master's in Learning Processes, from Our Lady of the Lake University in San Antonio in 2001. She is now working as the Crystal City High School librarian. Third, both of her sons have given her grandchildren. She lives for her grandkids now, she says.

I last interviewed her on March 28, 2004, to go over facts, dates, names, and the like. At that time, she asked me if I was returning to Crystal City, my hometown as well. I said it was very unlikely because I had no family there or property, just friends. She said, "You must. We still have a lot of work to do. I'd like to do some things here again."

Politics runs in her veins. Leadership is her calling. She is an inspiration and a role model. Severita Lara is a doer.

Severita's story can be heard from her own mouth and images of Severita may be viewed by visiting the Internet site www.libraries.uta.edu/tejanovoices.

Additional Hispanic Civil Rights Series titles

La Causa: Civil Rights, Social Justice and the Struggle for Equality in the Midwest

Edited by Gilberto Cárdenas
2004, 176 pages, Clothbound
ISBN 1-55885-425-8, $28.95

In the first text examining Latinos in the Midwest, social science scholars evaluate the efforts and progress toward social justice, examine such diverse topics as advocacy efforts, civil rights and community organizations, Latina Civil Rights efforts, ethnic diversity and political identity, effects of legislation for Homeland Security, and political empowerment. *La Causa* fills a gaping void in the literature available about the Civil Rights Movement in the Midwest.

". . . a fine collection of essays...This readable book details the often-neglected history of Latino and Mexican immigrant life in the Midwest, and would make a fine undergraduate course volume or reference work for student research projects." —*CHOICE*

Hector P. García: In Relentless Pursuit of Justice

Ignacio M. García
2002, 416 pages, Clothbound
ISBN 1-55885-387-1, $26.95

This first definitive, superbly researched and documented biography of the founder of the American GI Forum is an objective appraisal of his successes and failures, as well as an analysis of the political, social and personal issues that he and the American G.I. Forum confronted during his lifetime.

"The author . . . makes the case for his central role in the history of the struggle of Mexican Americans for a place in society . . ." —*MultiCultural Review*

Call toll free 1-800-633-ARTE to place your book order!

Message to Aztlán

Rodolfo "Corky" Gonzales
Foreword by Rodolfo F. Acuña
Edited, with an Introduction, by Antonio Esquibel
2001, 256 pages, Trade Paperback
ISBN 1-55885-331-6, $14.95

Message to Aztlán is the first collection of Rodolfo "Corky" Gonzales' diverse writings: *I Am Joaquín* (1967); seven major speeches (1968-78); two plays, *The Revolutionist* and *A Cross for Malcovio* (1966-67); various poems and a selection of letters. Eight pages of photographs accompany the text.

"Gonzales' poetry and plays . . . are historically important and represent the struggles encountered by Chicanos up to the 1980's." —*Library Journal*

"*Message to Aztlán* contains a valuable key to understanding the depths of Gonzales' revulsion to mainstream politics and its representatives." —*San Antonio Express-News*

Black Cuban, Black American: A Memoir

Evelio Grillo
Introduction by Kenya Dworkin-Mendez
2000, 224 pages, Trade Paperback
ISBN 1-55885-293-X, $13.95
Contains an eight page photo insert

Refer to the **Recovering the U.S. Hispanic Literary Heritage Series** section for a complete description.

A Chicano Manual on How to Handle Gringos

José Angel Gutiérrez
2003, 240 pages, Trade Paperback
ISBN 1-55885-396-0, $12.95

This manual penned by the founder of the only successful Hispanic political party, La Raza Unida, brings together an impressive breadth of models to either follow or avoid. This is a wonderful survey of the Chicano and Latino community on the move in all spheres of life in the United States on the very eve of its demographic and cultural ascendancy.

Additional Hispanic Civil Rights Series titles

A Gringo Manual on How to Handle Mexicans
José Angel Gutiérrez
2001, 160 pages, Trade Paperback
ISBN 1-55885-326-X, $12.95

Originally self-published during the heat of the Chicano Movement, this tongue-in-cheek guide now expanded and revised, is a humorous and irreverent manual meant to educate grass-roots leaders in practical strategies for community organization, leadership and negotiation. Gutiérrez attacks the authorities that caused Chicanos anxiety for decades.

"This is a classic in Chicano politics."
—*Pluma Fronteriza*

Memoir of a Visionary: Antonia Pantoja
Antonia Pantoja
Foreword by Henry A.J. Ramos
2002, 218 pages, Trade Paperback
ISBN 1-55885-385-5, $14.95

This compelling autobiography traces the trajectory of the groundbreaking Puerto Rican leader Antonia Pantoja, from a struggling school teacher in Puerto Rico to her work as principal engineer of the most enduring Puerto Rican organizations in New York City.

"A winner of the Presidential Medal of Freedom in 1996, Pantoja has crafted a sincere and politically illuminating autobiography that sticks to ways and means, and the complex encounters and emotions that accompany them." —*Publishers Weekly*

"This is an inspiring look at a community-spirited individual and the development of a grass-roots organization." —*Booklist*

"*Memoir of a Visionary* is a refreshing read, free of the false modesty that marks most such books."
—*Washington Post Book World*

The American GI Forum
In Pursuit of the Dream, 1948-1983
Henry Ramos
1998, 224 pages
Clothbound, ISBN 1-55885-261-1, $24.95
Trade Paperback, ISBN 1-55885-262-X, $14.95

This book traces the stormy history of one of U.S. Hispanics' most important but least known civil-rights groups—the American G.I. Forum—from its controversial inception through the presidency of Ronald Reagan.

"Ramos also provides a rarely seen glimpse of the politics of this minority group ... The writing is clear ... and the material will probably be new to most collections." —*School Library Journal*

Chicano! The History of the Mexican American Civil Rights Movement
F. Arturo Rosales
1997, 304 pages, Trade Paperback
ISBN 1-55885-201-8, $24.95

Recipient of the Gustavus Myers Center for the Study of Human Rights in North America Book Award

This is the companion volume to the critically acclaimed, four-part documentary series of the same title, which is now available on video from the Corporation for Public Broadcasting.

"The book is an education and inspiration; particularly, the moving chapter on the United Farm Workers and its founder and leader, César Chávez."—*Booklist*

"... a valuable historical summary of political activism of Latinos of Mexican descent ... The value of Rosales's book is enhanced by the use of interview transcripts done for the TV series. " —*Library Journal*

Testimonio: A Documentary History of the Mexican-American Struggle for Civil Rights
F. Arturo Rosales
2000, 448 pages, Trade Paperback
ISBN 1-55885-299-9, $22.95

Beginning with the early 1800s and extending to the modern era, Rosales collects illuminating documents that shed light on the Mexican-American quest for life, liberty, and justice. Documents include petitions, correspondence, government reports, political proclamations, newspaper items, congressional testimony, memoirs, and even international treaties.

Call
toll free
1-800-633-ARTE
to place your book order!

Visit us
on the web at
www.artepublicopress.com

Additional Hispanic Civil Rights Series titles

They Called Me "King Tiger" My Struggle for the Land and Our Rights

Reies López Tijerina
English translation by José Ángel Gutiérrez
2000, 256 pages, Trade Paperback
ISBN 1-55885-302-2, $14.95

In this autobiography, Reies López Tijerina, writes about his attempts to reclaim land grants, including his taking up arms against the authorities and spending time in the federal prison system.

"His compelling, often controversial, story brings to life a time of great turmoil and a major civil rights leader who has faded into obscurity." —*MultiCultural Review*

Eyewitness: A Filmmaker's Memoir of the Chicano Movement

Jesús Treviño
2001, 400 pages, Trade Paperback
ISBN 1-55885-349-9, $15.95

Coming of age during the turmoil of the sixties, noted filmmaker Jesús Salvador Treviño was on the spot to record the struggles to organize students and workers into the largest social and political movement in the history of Latino communities in the United States.

"Treviño's memoir covers his work as a filmmaker and activist who participated in and documented many of the more significant events of the Mexican-American civil rights movement." —*MultiCultural Review*

"To read the book is to get an inside look at many of the characters and events that shaped a movement that gripped much of the Southwest in the 1960s and 1970s." —*The Arizona Republic*

"His filmmaker's eye provides for a critical and poignant point of view." —*Hispanic*